# THE CHILDREN'S
# COLLECTION

# THE CHILDREN'S COLLECTION

## ALICE & JADE STARMORE

INTERWEAVE PRESS

## Photography
DREAMTEAM SCENARIO

## Models
SAM & MOLLY MACLEOD
ZOE MACPHERSON
ROBERT & DAVID SMITH
THOMAS STARMORE
LAURIE & AMY STEWART

## Editing, design & production
WINDFALL PRESS

## Charts & knitting illustrations
JADE STARMORE

## Colour reproduction & printing
DAI NIPPON PRINTING CO (HK) LTD

## Publisher

INTERWEAVE PRESS, INC.
201 East Fourth Street
Loveland, Colorado 80537, USA

## Library of Congress
## Cataloging-in-Publication Data

Starmore, Alice.
    The children's collection / Alice & Jade Starmore
        p. cm.
    ISBN 1–883010–80–2
    1. Knitting–Patterns. 2. Children's clothing. 3. Sweaters.
        I. Starmore, Jade.  II. Title.

TT825 .S7327 2000
746.43'20432--dc21                    99–085692

# CONTENTS

# FISH & ANCHORS

Dark brown is the river,
Golden is the sand.
It flows along for ever,
With trees on either hand.

Green leaves a-floating,
Castles of the foam,
Boats of mine a-boating —
Where will all come home?

On goes the river
And out past the mill,
Away down the valley,
Away down the hill.

Away down the river,
A hundred miles or more,
Other little children
Shall bring my boats ashore.

WHERE GO THE BOATS ?
From A CHILD'S GARDEN OF VERSES
by Robert Louis Stevenson

To fit approx age 2-3[4-5,6-7,8-9] years, or —
chest 54-56[58-61,63-66,68-71]cm
21-22[23-24,25-26,27-28]in.
Directions for larger sizes are given in square brackets.
Where there is only one set of figures, it applies to all
sizes.

### KNITTED MEASUREMENTS

Underarm 66[72,78,84]cm 26[28.5,31,33]in.
Length 31[34,39,43]cm. Sleeve Length 22[24,27,30]cm.

### MATERIALS

Of **Alice Starmore Scottish Campion** —
2 Skeins each of Goldenrod, Campbell Red and
Seabright. 1[2,2,2] Skeins of Leprechaun. 1[1,2,2]
Skeins each of Crimson and Forget-Me-Not.
1 Set of double-pointed or circular 2.75mm (US 2) and
3.25mm (US 3) needles. **Note:** A set of short double-
pointed needles in each size will also be required to
work the lower sleeves, cuffs and neckband.
2 Stitch holders. 2 Safety pins. Stitch markers.

### STITCHES

**2/2 Rib:** K2 with first colour, p2 with second colour,
stranding the yarns evenly across the WS. **Chart Patt:**
All rnds are read from right to left. K every rnd stranding the yarn not in immediate use evenly across the WS.
**Steeks:** Worked at armholes and front and back neck,
and later cut up centre to form openings. Each steek is
worked over 8 sts and on two-colour rnds, k in alt
colours on every st and rnd. Do not weave in newly
joined in or broken off yarns at centre of first armhole
steek. Instead leave approx 5cm tail when joining in and
breaking off yarns. **Edge St:** Worked at each side of
steeks and K in background colours throughout. Sts for
sleeves and neckband are knitted up from edge st.
**Cross Stitch:** With tapestry needle, overcast trimmed
steeks to strands on WS, and after sewing to end, reverse
to form cross sts.

### TENSION

30 Sts and 34 rows to 10cm, measured over chart patt
using 3.25mm needles. To make an accurate tension
swatch, cast on 36 sts on 1 double-pointed or circular
needle and rep the 18 patt sts twice, **knitting on the
right side only**, breaking of the yarns at the end of
every row. Read all rows from right to left and beg at row
1, patt 36 rows.

FISH & ANCHORS is a traditionally styled
pullover knitted entirely in the round, with
steeks worked at the armholes and neck.
While a complete newcomer to 'steek technique' may wish to start out with a sleeveless
garment such as ELEPHANTS, this is an ideal
exercise for any knitter wishing to become
familiar with the traditional dropped shoulder
style of Fair Isle pullover. A novice at knitting
steeks should look at the brief outline of the
technique on P31, or for more detail, consult
ALICE STARMORE'S BOOK OF FAIR ISLE
KNITTING. Practised Fair Isle knitters will
find FISH & ANCHORS straight-forward.

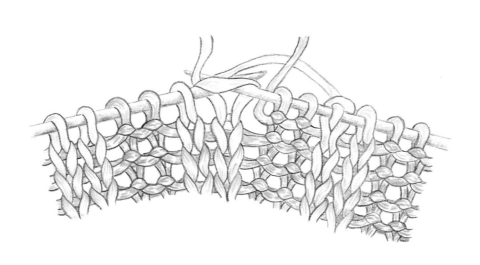

In FISH & ANCHORS you will work coloured 2/2 rib on the lower body, neckband and cuffs. The knit stitches are worked in one colour and the purl stitches in another. Remember to bring the yarn to the BACK of the work after each p2, as shown in the drawing above.

## BODY

With 2.75mm needles and Leprechaun, cast on 188[204,220,236]sts. Place a marker at beg of rnd and making sure cast on edge is not twisted, join in and break off colours as required and work 13[15,15,15]rnds of 2/2 rib as follows—
**4[5,5,5] Rnds** of k2 Leprechaun, p2 Crimson. **1 Rnd** of k2 Seabright, p2 Crimson. **4 Rnds** of k2 Seabright, p2 Campbell Red. **1 Rnd** of k2 Forget-Me-Not, p2 Campbell Red. **3[4,4,4] Rnds** of k2 Forget-Me-Not, p2 Goldenrod. With Goldenrod inc on next rnd as follows—
**First, Third & Fourth Sizes:** K 8[10,12]; * m1, k 18[15,14]; rep from * to end of rnd. 198[234,252] Sts.
**Second Size:** * M1, k17; rep from * to end of rnd. 216 Sts.
**All Sizes:** Change to 3.25mm needles, place a marker at beg of rnd and joining in and breaking off colours as required, beg at rnd 1[1,1,24] of chart and set the patt as follows—
**First and Third Sizes:** Patt the last 9 sts of rep; rep the 18 patt sts 10[12] times; patt first 9 sts of rep.
**Second and Fourth Sizes:** Rep the 18 patt sts 12[14] times.
**All Sizes:** Continue as set and work 46[50,60,67] chart patt rnds, thus ending on rnd 46[4,14,44] inclusive. Break off yarns.
**Next Rnd – Work Armhole Steeks and Edge Sts**
Place the first st of rnd on a safety pin; with Goldenrod[alt,alt,alt] colours as for next rnd of chart, cast on 4 steek sts and mark the first st cast on for beg of rnd; with Goldenrod[Goldenrod, Goldenrod, Forget-Me-Not] cast on 1 edge st; keeping continuity, patt the next rnd of chart over the next 98[107,116,125] sts (front); place the next st on a safety pin; with colour(s) as before cast on 1 edge st; cast on 8 steek sts; cast on 1 edge st; keeping continuity, patt the the rem 98[107,116,125] sts (back); with colour(s) as before cast on 1 edge st; cast on 4 steek sts. Work steek sts in alt colours on two-colour rnds and edge sts in background colours throughout, and continue in patt as set over the front and back sts until 73[78,94,106] chart patt rnds

have been worked from beg, thus ending on rnd 27[32,2,37] inclusive.

### Next Rnd – Beg Front Neck Shaping

With colours as for next rnd of chart, k4 steek sts and k1 edge st as set; keeping continuity, patt the first 36[40,44,47] sts; place the next 26[27,28,31] sts on a holder; with background colour cast on 1 edge st; with alt colours cast on 8 steek sts; with background colour cast on 1 edge st; keeping continuity, patt as set to end of rnd. K edge sts in background colours throughout, and k steek sts in alt colours on two-colour rnds and keeping continuity of patt, dec 1 st at chart patt side of front neck edge sts on next 3[3,4,2] rnds, then on every foll alt rnd 4[5,5,7] times in all. 29[32,35,38] Chart patt sts rem on each front shoulder. Patt 1 rnd without shaping.

### Next Rnd – Beg Back Neck Shaping

Keeping continuity of patt, dec 1 st as set at each side of front neck edge – 28[31,34,37] chart patt sts rem on each front shoulder; then continue as set to the 98[107,116,125] chart patt sts of back; patt the first 30[33,36,39] sts as set; place the next 38[41,44,47] sts on a holder; cast on 10 steek and edge sts as front neck; keeping continuity, patt to end of rnd. Keeping continuity of patt, dec 1 st at chart patt side of back neck edge sts on next 2 rnds – 28[31,34,37] chart patt sts rem on each shoulder. Patt 2 rnds without shaping and cast off all steek sts on last rnd, ending on rnd 45[6,23,14] inclusive. With Forget-Me-Not [Goldenrod, Crimson, Goldenrod] graft sts together including edge sts.

## SLEEVES

Cut open armhole steeks up centre between 4th and 5th steek sts.

With 3.25mm needles and Forget-Me-Not [Goldenrod, Goldenrod, Crimson], k the st from safety pin and mark this st for beg of rnd and underarm st; knit up 77[85,97,109] sts evenly around armhole, working into loop of edge st next to chart patt sts. 78[86,98,110] Sts. Turn chart upside down and joining in and breaking off colours as required, beg at rnd 46[6,15,23] of chart and set the patt as follows—

With background colour k underarm st; reading from right to left in upside down position, patt the last 3[7,4,1] sts of rep; rep the 18 patt sts 4[4,5,6] times; patt the first 2[6,3,0] sts of rep.

Working back through the chart rnds patt the next 3 rnds as set, working the underarm st in background colours throughout.

### Next Rnd – Begin Sleeve Shaping

With colours as for next rnd of chart, k the underarm st; k2tog in background colour; keeping continuity, patt to the last 2 sts; ssk in background colour. Working back through the chart and keeping continuity, patt 3 rnds without shaping. Rep these 4 rnds until 50[54,68,84] sts rem.

**Third & Fourth Sizes:** Keeping continuity of patt, dec as set on next and every foll 3rd rnd until 58[62] sts rem.

**All Sizes:** 58[65,75,85] Chart patt rnds worked in total, thus ending on rnd 35[30,33,31] inclusive.

### Next Rnd – Dec for Cuff

With Seabright[Goldenrod,Leprechaun,Leprechaun] – k 2[0,4,2]; * k2tog, k 6[7,7,8]; rep from * to end of rnd. 44[48,52,56] Sts rem. Change to 2.75mm needles and work 15 rnds of 2/2 rib as follows—

**4 Rnds** of k2 Forget-Me-Not, p2 Goldenrod. **1 Rnd** of k2 Forget-Me-Not, p2 Campbell Red. **4 Rnds** of k2 Seabright, p2 Campbell Red. **1 Rnd** of k2 Seabright, p2 Crimson. **5 Rnds** of k2 Leprechaun, p2 Crimson. With Leprechaun, cast off knitwise.

### Neckband

Cut open front and back neck steeks up centre between 4th and 5th steek sts. With RS facing, 2.75mm needles and Forget-Me-Not, beg at back neck holder and pick up sts as follows —

Pick up and k the 38[41,44,47] sts from back neck holder; knit up 18[20,22,23] sts evenly along left side of neck working into loop of edge sts next to chart patt sts; pick up and k the 26[27,28,31] sts from front neck holder; knit up 18[20,22,23] sts evenly along right side of neck, working into edge sts as before. 100[108,116,124] Sts. Place a marker at beg of rnd and work 8 rnds of 2/2 rib as follows —

**2 Rnds** of k2 Forget-Me-Not, p2 Goldenrod. **1 Rnd** of k2 Seabright, p2 Goldenrod. **2 Rnds** of k2 Seabright, p2 Campbell Red. **1 Rnd** of k2 Leprechaun, p2 Campbell Red. **2 Rnds** of k2 Leprechaun, p2 Crimson. With Leprechaun cast off knitwise.

## FINISHING

Trim all steeks to a 2 stitch width and with Goldenrod, cross stitch steeks in position. Darn in all loose ends. Using a warm iron and damp cloth, press garment lightly on WS omitting ribs.

## CHART A

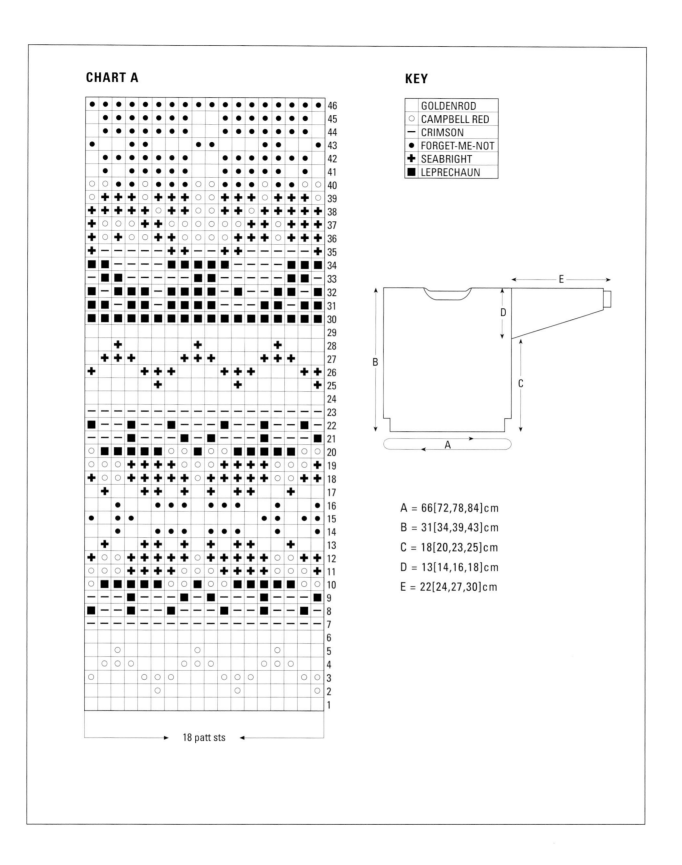

**KEY**

| | |
|---|---|
| | GOLDENROD |
| ○ | CAMPBELL RED |
| — | CRIMSON |
| ● | FORGET-ME-NOT |
| ✛ | SEABRIGHT |
| ■ | LEPRECHAUN |

18 patt sts

A = 66[72,78,84]cm

B = 31[34,39,43]cm

C = 18[20,23,25]cm

D = 13[14,16,18]cm

E = 22[24,27,30]cm

# CHILD'S MENDOCINO

She looked up at the Queen, who seemed to have suddenly wrapped herself up in wool. Alice rubbed her eyes, and looked again. She couldn't make out what had happened at all. Was she in a shop? And was that really — was it really a sheep that was sitting on the other side of the counter? Rub as she would, she could make nothing more of it: she was in a little dark shop, leaning with her elbows on the counter, and opposite to her was an old Sheep, sitting in an arm-chair, knitting, and every now and then leaving off to look at her through a great pair of spectacles.

"What is it you want to buy?" the Sheep said at last, looking up for a moment from her knitting.

"I don't quite know yet," Alice said very gently. "I should like to look all round me first, if I might."

"You may look in front of you, and on both sides, if you like," said the Sheep; "but you can't look all round you — unless you've got eyes at the back of your head."

But these, as it happened, Alice had not got: so she contented herself with turning round, looking at the shelves as she came to them.

The shop seemed to be full of all manner of curious things — but the oddest part of it all was that, whenever she looked hard at any shelf, to make out what it had on it, that particular shelf was always quite empty, though the others round it were crowded as full as they could hold.

"Things flow about so here!" she said at last in a plaintive tone...

From THROUGH THE LOOKING GLASS by Lewis Carroll

MENDOCINO was originally designed as a woman's garment and proved to be hugely popular. It is elegant – and versatile since it can be worn casually or formally – yet very easy to knit. The pictures on these and the following pages show how colour choice can alter the mood of the garment and adapt it to many different circumstances.

To fit age 2-3[4-5,6-7,8-9] years, or — chest 54-56[58-61,63-66,68-71]cm 21-22[23-24,25-26,27-28]in. Directions for larger sizes are given in square brackets. Where there is only one set of figures, it applies to all sizes.

## KNITTED MEASUREMENTS

Underarm (buttoned) 85[90,95,99]cm 33[35.5,37.5,39]in.
Length 42[48,56,62]cm.
Sleeve length 24[27,30,33]cm.

## MATERIALS

3[4,6,7] Skeins of **Alice Starmore Bainin** shown in Ecru, Mulberry and Spruce.
1 pair each of 4mm (US 6) and 5mm (US 8) needles.
1 Cable needle. 5 Stitch holders. 6[7,8,9] Buttons.

## STITCHES

**Stocking Stitch (St.st):** K all RS rows. P all WS rows. Work Edgings and collar in **either** Moss Stitch **or** Seed Stitch according to preference.
**Moss Stitch:** Worked over an odd number of sts as follows—
**Rows 1 & 4:** * K1, p1; rep from * to the last st; k1.
**Rows 2 & 3:** * P1, k1; rep from * to the last st; p1. Rep rows 1 – 4.
**Seed Stitch:** Worked over an odd number of sts as follows—
**All Rows:** * K1, p1; rep from * to the last st; k1.
**Chart Patt:** All odd numbered rows are RS and are read from right to left. All even numbered rows are WS and are read from left to right.

## TENSION

19 Sts and 24 rows to 10cm, measured over St.st using 5mm needles.

## RIGHT FRONT

With 5mm needles, cast on 37[39,41,43] sts. Work 8 rows of Moss or Seed Stitch.
**Next Row (RS) – Inc**
K10[12,14,16]; (m1, k10) twice; work Moss/Seed stitch as set over the last 7 sts. 39[41,43,45] Sts. Set the patt as follows—
**Row 1 (WS):** Work Moss/Seed Stitch as set over the first 7 sts; p 32[34,36,38].
**Row 2 (RS):** K 32[34,36,38]; work Moss/Seed Stitch as set over the last 7 sts.
Rep these last 2 rows until front measures 7[8,9,10]cm from cast on edge, with WS facing for next row. Beginning with a p row continue in St.st over all sts until front measures 25[29,32,36]cm from cast on edge with RS facing for next row.

**Set Right Yoke Patt**

**Row 1 (RS):** K1; reading from right to left, rep the 7 patt sts 2[2,3,3] times; patt the last 2 sts as indicated; k 22[24,19,21].

**Row 2 (WS):** P 22[24,19,21]; reading from left to right, patt the first 2 sts as indicated; rep the 7 patt sts 2[2,3,3] times; p1.

Continue as set and work through row 10 of chart once only. Thereafter rep rows 7 through 10 until front measures 35[41,48,54]cm from cast on edge with RS facing for next row.

**Shape front Neck**

+ Patt the first 5[6,7,8] sts and place these sts on a holder; keeping continuity, patt to end of row. Keeping continuity as far as possible throughout, dec 1 st at neck edge of next 2 rows, then dec 1 st at neck edge of every foll alt row 4 times in all. 28[29,30,31] Sts rem. ++ Patt 1[1,3,3] rows without shaping. Cast off all sts in patt and dec 1 st over cable during cast off.

## LEFT FRONT

Cast on 37[39,41,43] sts and work 8 rows of Moss/Seed Stitch as right front.

**Next Row (RS) – Inc**

Work Moss/Seed Stitch as set over the first 7 sts; (k10, m1) twice; k 10[12,14,16]. 39[41,43,45] Sts. Continue as right front but work Moss/Seed Stitch edging at right side as set in the previous row. Work edging and change to St.st as right front and continue until left front matches right front in length to beg of yoke patt, with RS facing for next row.

**Set Left Yoke Patt**

**Row 1 (RS):** K 22[24,19,21]; reading from right to left rep the 7 patt sts 2[2,3,3] times; patt the last 2 sts as indicated; k1.

**Row 2 (WS):** P1; reading from left to right, patt the first 2 sts as indicated; rep the 7 patt sts 2[2,3,3] times; p 22[24,19,21].

Continue as set, working rows 1 through 10 of chart once only. Thereafter rep rows 7 through 10 until left front matches right front in length, plus 1 extra row, thus ending with WS facing for next row. Shape left neck as right from + to ++.

**Third & Fourth Sizes Only:** Patt 2 rows without shaping.

**All Sizes:** Cast off the rem 28[29,30,31] sts as right front.

## BACK

With 5mm needles, cast on 77[81,85,89] sts. Work Moss/Seed Stitch for 8 rows.

**Next Row (RS) – Inc**

Work Moss/Seed Stitch as set over the first 7 sts; k 4[6,5,7]; * m1; k 18[18,20,20]; rep from * 3 times in all; m1; k 5[7,6,8]; work Moss/Seed Stitch as set over the last 7 sts. 81[85,89,93] Sts.

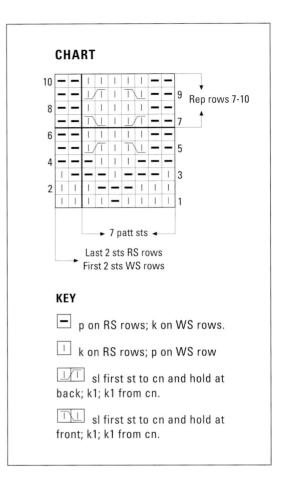

**CHART**

→ 7 patt sts ←

Last 2 sts RS rows
First 2 sts WS rows

Rep rows 7-10

**KEY**

⊟ p on RS rows; k on WS rows.

▯ k on RS rows; p on WS row

⧄ sl first st to cn and hold at back; k1; k1 from cn.

⧅ sl first st to cn and hold at front; k1; k1 from cn.

Beg with a WS row and work Moss/Seed Stitch as set over the first and last 7 sts and work St.st over the inside 67[71,75,79] sts until back measures 7[8,9,10]cm from cast on edge with WS facing for next row.

Beg with a p row and continue in St. St. over all sts until back matches fronts in length to beg of yoke patt, with RS facing for next row.

**Set Back Yoke Patt**

**Row 1 (RS):** K 22[24,19,21]; reading from right to left, rep the 7 patt sts 5[5,7,7] times; patt the last 2 sts as indicated; k 22[24,19,21].

**Row 2 (WS):** P 22[24,19,21]; reading from left to right, patt the first 2 sts as indicated; rep the 7 patt sts 5[5,7,7] times; p 22[24,19,21].

Continue as set, working rows 1 through 10 of chart once only. Thereafter rep rows 7 through 10 until back matches fronts in length at shoulder cast off edge, with RS facing for next row.

**Shape Shoulders**

Cast off 28[29,30,31] sts at beg of next 2 rows and dec 1 st over cables during cast off. Place the centre back 25[27,29,31] sts on a holder.

## SLEEVES

With 4mm needles, cast on 36[38,40,42] sts. Work k1, p1 rib for 4[4.5,5,5]cm, with WS facing for next row.

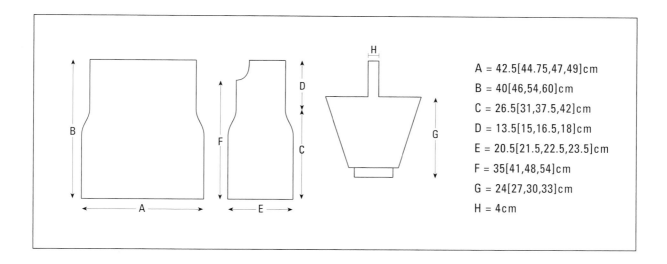

A = 42.5[44.75,47,49]cm

B = 40[46,54,60]cm

C = 26.5[31,37.5,42]cm

D = 13.5[15,16.5,18]cm

E = 20.5[21.5,22.5,23.5]cm

F = 35[41,48,54]cm

G = 24[27,30,33]cm

H = 4cm

## Next Row – Inc

Rib 2[3,2,3]; * m1; rib 8[8,6,6]; rep from * to the last 2[3,2,3] sts; m1; rib 2[3,2,3]. 41[43,47,49] Sts.

Change to 5mm needles and beg with a RS row, work all sts in St.st and inc 1 st at each end of 3rd row, working inc sts in St.st. Then continue as set and inc 1 st at each end of every foll 4th row until sleeve measures 14[17,20,23]cm from cast on edge with RS facing for next row.

## Set Chart Patt

Continue to work in St.st at each side and continue to inc on every 4th row as set. AT THE SAME TIME, work the chart patt over the centre 23 sts as follows—

**Row 1 (RS):** Reading from right to left, rep the 7 patt sts 3 times; patt the last 2 sts as indicated.

**Row 2 (WS):** Reading from left to right, patt the first 2 sts as indicated; rep the 7 patt sts 3 times.

Continue as set, working rows 1 through 10 once only. Thereafter rep rows 7 through 10. Continue to inc at each end of every 4th row until there are 63[69,75,81] sts in total, then continue as set without further shaping until sleeve measures 24[27,30,33]cm from cast on edge, with RS facing for next row.

## Shape Saddle

Cast off 27[30,33,36] sts at beg of next 2 rows, decreasing 1 st over cables during cast off. 9 Centre sleeve sts rem.

Continue in patt as set over the 9 rem sts until saddle fits in length along shoulder cast off edges. Place sts on a holder.

### FINISHING

Using a warm iron and a damp cloth, press the WS of St.st area of each piece. Do not press cabled areas, thus allowing the cable patt to gather the shape in gently on yokes and sleeves. Place markers 13.5[15,16.5,18]cm down from shoulder cast off edge on back and fronts. Sew saddles along shoulder cast off edges of back and fronts. Sew cast off edges of sleeves to back and fronts between markers. Press seams on WS using the edge of the iron, thus avoiding pressing on cable areas. Sew up side seams from top of Moss/Seed Stitch edgings. Sew up sleeve seams. Press seams on WS omitting ribs.

## Collar

With RS facing and 4mm needles, beg at right front and pick up and k the 5[6,7,8] sts from holder; knit up 10[10,12,12] sts evenly along right side of neck; pick up and k the 9 sts from right saddle and dec 1 st at centre of cable; pick up and k the 25[27,29,31] sts from back neck holder; pick up and k the 9 sts from left saddle and dec 1 st at centre of cable; knit up 10[10,12,12] sts along left side of neck; pick up and k the 5[6,7,8] sts from front neck holder. 71[75,83,87] Sts.

### Rib as follows—

**Row 1 (WS):** P1; * k1, p1; rep from * to end of row.

**Row 2 (RS):** K1; *p1, k1: rep from * to end of row.

Rep these 2 rows and work 6[6,8,8] rows in total.

Change to 5mm needles and work 15[17,19,21] rows of Moss/Seed Stitch. Cast off in patt.

## Button Band

With 4mm needles, cast on 7 sts. Work Moss/Seed Stitch until band, when slightly stretched, fits along left front edge to top of collar rib. Cast off sts. Pin and sew front band to front edge. Mark position of 6[7,8,9] buttons on band with pins to ensure even spacing, the first to come 7cm from cast on edge (bottom), the last to come 1.5cm from cast off edge (top), with the rem spaced evenly between.

## Buttonhole Band

Work as button band with the addition of 6[7,8,9] buttonholes, worked to correspond with markers on button band. Work buttonholes as follows—

**Buttonhole Row:** Moss Stitch 3; yo, patt 2 tog; Moss Stitch 2.

Pin and sew band in position as button band. Press seams lightly on WS, avoiding pressing on yoke cables. Sew buttons on to button band.

In the pattern for MENDOCINO you will find an option for two slightly different stitches on the collar and edgings. The choice is either Moss Stitch or Seed Stitch. Here you see Laurie and Thomas both wearing the Moss Stitch version, which gives a softer texture. This design really is versatile. It looks wonderful on a young girl dressed up for a smart occasion, yet looks equally good on highly active small boys up to the age of around four years.

Here you see Zoe wearing the Seed Stitch version which has a crisp texture. In the back view (ABOVE LEFT) you can see how the cabled centre yoke pattern gently gathers the garment. This is an important feature of the design which can be spoiled by over-enthusiastic pressing at the finishing stage. All cabled areas of the design should be left unpressed. The centre sleeve cable is continued to form a narrow saddle. Here you must take care to use only the edge of the iron to press the saddle seams, thus avoiding pressing on the cable itself.

# ORIENTAL FLOWER

ORIENTAL FLOWER is an easy-to-knit cardigan in exotic colours, worked in the round, with steeks at front and armholes. Molly is photographed in her seaside garden on the Isle of Harris.

It was the birthday of the Infanta. She was just twelve years of age, and the sun was shining brightly in the gardens of the palace.

Although she was a real Princess and the Infanta of Spain, she had only one birthday every year, just like the children of quite poor people, so it was naturally a matter of great importance to the whole country that she should have a really fine day for the occasion. And a really fine day it certainly was. The tall striped tulips looked straight up upon their stalks, like a long row of soldiers, and looked defiantly across the grass at the roses, and said: "We are quite as splendid as you are now." The purple butterflies fluttered about with gold dust on their wings, visiting each flower in turn; the little lizards crept out of crevices in the wall, and lay basking in the white glare; and the pomegranates split and cracked with the heat, and showed their bleeding red hearts. Even the pale yellow lemons, that hung in such profusion from the mouldering trellis and along the dim arcades, seemed to have caught a richer colour from the wonderful sunlight, and the magnolia trees opened their great globe-like blossoms of folded ivory, and filled the air with a sweet heavy perfume.

From THE BIRTHDAY OF THE INFANTA
by Oscar Wilde

To fit age approx 2-3[4-5,6-7,8-9] years, or —
chest 54-56[58-61,63-66,68-71]cm
21-22[23-24,25-26,27-28]in. Directions for larger sizes
are given in square brackets. Where there is only one set
of figures, it applies to all sizes.

## KNITTED MEASUREMENTS

Underarm (buttoned) 68[73,80,86]cm 27[29,31.5,34]in.
Length 35[38,44,47]cm.
Sleeve length 23[26,29,33]cm.

## MATERIALS

Of **Alice Starmore Scottish Campion** —
2 Skeins each of Verdigris, Delph and Crimson. 1[1,2,2]
Skeins each of Campbell Red and Pumpkin. 1 Skein
each of Gold, Cobalt and Sea Pink.
1 Set of double-pointed or circular 2.75mm (US 2) and
3.25mm (US 3) needles. **Note:** A set of short double-
pointed needles in each size will also be required to
work the lower sleeves.
1 Stitch holder. 2 Safety pins. 5[5,6,6] Buttons.

## STITCHES

**Chart Patts:** All rnds are read from right to left. K every
rnd, stranding the yarn not in immediate use evenly
across the WS. **Steeks:** Worked at front and armholes
and later cut up centre to form openings. Each steek is
worked over 8 sts. On two-colour rnds the steek sts are
worked in alt colours on every st and rnd. Do not weave
in newly joined in and broken off yarns at the centre of
front steek. Instead leave approx. 5cm tail when joining
in and breaking off yarns. **Edge Stitch:** Worked at each
side of steeks and k in background colours throughout.
Sts for sleeves and bands are knitted up from edge sts.
**Cross Stitch:** With tapestry needle, overcast raw edges
of trimmed steeks to strands on WS. After sewing to end
reverse to form cross stitches.

## TENSION

30 Sts and 34 rows to 10cm, measured over chart patt
using 3.25mm needles. To make an accurate tension
swatch, cast on 42 sts on 1 double-pointed or circular
needle and rep the 14 patt sts of chart A 3 times. Work a
flat piece, **knitting on the RS only**, breaking off the
yarns at the end of every row.

## BODY

With a set of double-pointed or circular 2.75mm
needles and Crimson, cast on 206[224,244,262] sts.
Place a marker at beg of rnd and making sure cast on
edge is not twisted k 9 rnds.

**Next Rnd – Hemline**
K5; p to the last 5 sts; k5.
With Crimson k 1 rnd (rnd 6 of charts).
**Set Chart Patts**
Change to 3.25mm needles, join in Gold and reading
from right to left, beg at rnd 7 of charts and set the patt
as follows —
**First & Fourth Sizes:** With alt colours k4 steek sts; with
Crimson k1 edge st; rep the 14 patt sts of Chart A 7[9]
times; rep the 14 patt sts of chart B 7[9] times; with
Crimson k1 edge st; with alt colours k4 steek sts.
**Second & Third Sizes:** With alt colours k4 steek sts;
with Crimson k1 edge st; patt the last 9[5] sts of chart A;
rep the 14 patt sts of chart A 7[8] times; rep the 14 sts of
chart B 7[8] times; patt the first 9[5] sts of chart B; with
Crimson k1 edge st; with alt colours k4 steek sts.

**All Sizes**
Joining in and breaking off colours as required, and
working steek sts in alt colours on two-colour rnds and
edge sts in background colours throughout, work
through the chart patt rnds until 74[80,96,100] rnds
have been worked from hemline rnd, thus ending on
rnd 17[23,8,12] inclusive of charts.
**Next Rnd – Beg Armhole Steeks**
With colours as set for next rnd of charts, k4 steek sts
and k1 edge st as set; patt the next 47[51,56,61] sts as
set (right front); place the next st on a safety pin; with
colours as set, cast on 1 edge st; cast on 8 steek sts; cast
on 1 edge st; keeping continuity patt the next
100[110,120,128] sts (back); place the next st on a
safety pin; cast on 10 steek and edge sts as before;
keeping continuity patt the next 47[51,56,61] sts as set
(left front); k1 edge st and k4 steek sts as set.
Continue as set, working armhole steeks in alt colours
on two-colour rnds and edge sts in background colours
throughout. Work a further 3[5,6,10] rnds, thus ending
on rnd 21[29,15,23] inclusive of charts.
**Next Rnd – Beg Front Neck Shaping**
With colours as set for next rnd of charts, k4 steek sts
and k1 edge st as set; ssk and place a marker for beg of
V neck; keeping continuity patt straight as set to the last
7 sts; k2tog and place a marker for beg of V neck; k1
edge st and k4 steek sts as set.
Keeping continuity of patt, dec 1 st as set on chart patt
side of front neck edge sts on the next 4[4,5,7] rnds.
42[46,50,53] Chart patt sts rem on each front.
Patt 1 rnd without shaping. Keeping continuity of patt,
dec 1 st on chart patt side of front neck edge sts on next
and every foll alt rnd until 37[41,45,47] chart patt sts
rem on each front shoulder.
Patt 2 rnds without shaping. Keeping continuity of patt,
dec 1 st on chart patt side of front neck edge sts on next
and every foll 3rd rnd until 33[37,41,45] chart patt sts
rem on each front shoulder.

## CHART A

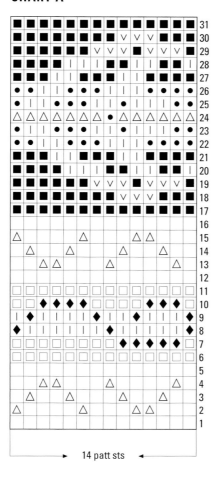

← 14 patt sts →

## CHART B

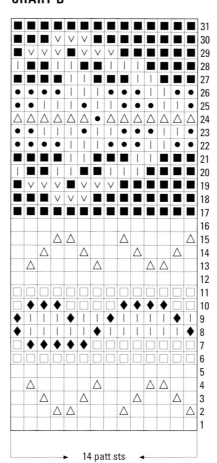

← 14 patt sts →

## KEY

| | |
|---|---|
| ☐ | VERDIGRIS |
| △ | PUMPKIN |
| ☐ | CRIMSON |
| ◆ | GOLD |
| I | CAMPBELL RED |
| ■ | DELPH |
| V | SEA PINK |
| ● | COBALT |

A = 68[73,80,86]cm

B = 35[38,44,47]cm

C = 22[23.5,28,29]cm

D = 13[14.5,16,18]cm

E = 23[26,29,33]cm

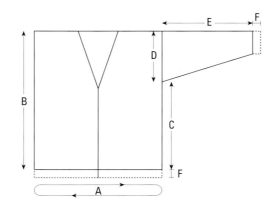

Patt 3 rnds without shaping. Keeping continuity of patt, dec 1 st on chart patt side of front neck edge sts on next and every foll 4th rnd until 30[34,37,40] chart patt sts rem on each front shoulder.

Patt 1[4,2,3] rnds without shaping. 118[129,149,160] Rnds of charts A and B worked in total from beg, thus ending on rnd 30[10,30,10] inclusive.

**Next Rnd:** Cast off first 4 steek sts; k1 edge st as set; patt the next 30[34,37,40] sts as set (right front); k1 edge st as set; cast off 8 steek sts; k1 edge st as set; patt the first 30[34,37,40] sts of back as set; patt the next 40[42,46,48] sts and place these sts on a holder for back neck; patt the last 30[34,37,40] sts of back as set; k1 edge st as set; cast off 8 steek sts; patt the next 30[34,37,40] sts as set (left front); k1 edge st as set; cast off 4 steek sts.

With Delph[Crimson,Delph,Crimson] graft front and back shoulders together including edge sts.

## SLEEVES

Cut open armhole steeks up centre between 4th and 5th steek sts.

With 3.25mm needles and Delph[Delph,Crimson,Cobalt] k the st from safety pin and mark this st for beg of rnd and underarm st; knit up 78[86,96,108] sts evenly around armhole, working into loop of edge st next to chart patt sts. 79[87,97,109] Sts.

Turn charts upside down and joining in and breaking off colours as required, beg at rnd 21[31,11,24] and set the patt as follows—

With background colour k underarm st; reading from right to left in upside down position, patt the last 11[1,6,12] sts of Chart A; rep the 14 patt sts of chart A 2[3,3,3] times; rep the 14 patt sts of chart B 2[3,3,3] times; patt the first 11[1,6,12] sts of chart B.

Working back through the chart rnds, patt the next 4[6,5,6] rnds as set, working the underarm st in background colours throughout.

**Next Rnd – Beg Sleeve Shaping**

With colours as for next rnd of chart, k the underarm st as set; k2tog; keeping continuity patt to the last 2 sts; ssk.

Keeping continuity, patt 3 rnds without shaping. Rep these last 4 rnds until 41[45,49,55] sts rem, thus working 78[88,99,112] rnds of charts from beg and ending on rnd 6 inclusive.

Change to a set of short 2.75mm needles.

**Next Rnd – Hemline**

With Crimson purl. With Crimson k 9 rnds. Cast off knitwise.

**Front Band**

Cut open front steek up centre, between 4th and 5th steek sts. With 3.25mm needles and Crimson, knit up into loop of edge st next to chart patt sts as follows — Beg at hemline (p rnd) of right front and knit up 69[76,91,98] sts evenly to V neck marker; knit up 37[40,42,45] sts evenly along right neck to back neck holder; pick up and k the 40[42,44,48] sts from holder; knit up 37[40,42,45] sts evenly along left neck to V neck marker; knit up 69[76,91,98] sts evenly to left front hemline. 252[274,310,334] Sts.

Working back and forth in rows, p1 row in Crimson. Join in Gold and beg at row 7 of charts and set the patt as follows —

**Next Row (RS):** Reading from right to left, and working all sts in k, patt the last 0[11,1,13] sts of chart A; rep the 14 patt sts of chart A 9[9,11,11] times; rep the 14 patt sts of chart B 9[9,11,11] times; patt the first 0[11,1,13] sts of chart B.

**Next Row (WS):** Reading from left to right, and working all sts in p, patt the last 0[11,1,13] sts of chart B; rep the 14 patt sts of chart B 9[9,11,11] times; rep the 14 patt sts of chart A 9[9,11,11] times; patt the first 0[11,1,13] sts of chart A.

**Next Row (RS) – Make Buttonholes**

Working row 9 of charts, patt 5[4,7,4] sts; *cast off 2, patt 13[15,14,16]; rep from * 4[4,5,5] times in all; cast of 2; patt as set to end of row.

On next row, keeping continuity of patt, cast on 2 sts over those cast off. Work through row 11 of charts A and B.

**Next Row (WS):** With Crimson purl. Change to 2.75mm needles.

**Next Row (RS) – Hemline:** With Crimson Purl. With Crimson work St.st (k RS rows, p WS rows) for 3 rows. On next row make 5[5,6,6] buttonholes as before and on foll row cast on 2 sts over those cast off. Continue in St.st until facing reaches band pick up line when folded at hemline. Cast off with a 3.25mm needle.

## FINISHING

Trim all steeks to a 2 stitch width and with Crimson, cross stitch steeks in position. Darn in all loose ends. Using a warm iron and damp cloth, press garment very lightly on WS. Fold all facings at hemlines and press lightly. Using Crimson catch stitch facings to WS. Sew buttons on to left front band.

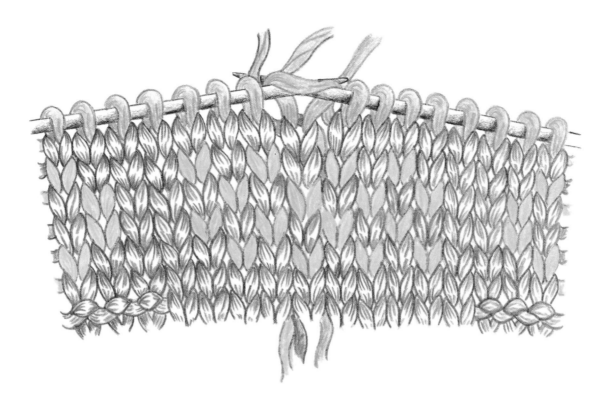

This drawing shows the front steek of ORIENTAL FLOWER being knitted. Ten stitches are required to work the steek and edge stitches. These 10 sts are made up of 8 actual steek sts with 1 edge st at either side. THEY ARE INCLUDED IN THE CAST-ON NUMBER GIVEN AT THE BEGINNING OF THE PATTERN. For example: if you are making the first size, the 206 sts cast on include the 8 steek and 2 edge sts. As the 9 rounds of the hem are worked in one colour only, the steek and edge sts do not become apparent until you have knitted the hemline round. In this round, the first and last 5 sts are worked in k while all the others are worked in p. The colour pattern begins after the hemline round. From then on, the 2 edge sts (shown by arrows in the drawing) are always worked in the background colour, while the 8 steek sts are worked in alternating colours on every two-colour round. Colour changes take place at the centre of the front steek. The drawing shows a new colour being joined in at the centre. There is no need to darn in yarn ends when joining in and breaking off colours. Simply leave them hanging, as they will be cut off later when the steek is finished. Refer to pages 100 to 104 of ALICE STARMORE'S BOOK OF FAIR ISLE KNITTING if you require a more comprehensive description of the steek technique.

# WESTERN SEAS

THEY SAILED to the Western Sea, they did, To a land all covered with trees, And they bought an Owl, and a useful Cart, And a pound of Rice and a Cranberry Tart, And a hive of silvery Bees. And they bought a Pig, and some green Jackdaws, And a lovely Monkey with lollipop paws, And forty bottles of Ring-Bo-Ree, And no end of Stilton cheese. Far and few, far and few, Are the lands where the Jumblies live; Their heads are green, and their hands are blue, And they went to sea in a Sieve.

AND IN twenty years they all came back, In twenty years or more, And everyone said, "How tall they've grown! For they've been to the Lakes and the Terrible Zone, And the hills of the Chankly Bore." And they drank their health, and gave them a feast Of dumplings made of beautiful yeast; And everyone said, "If we only live, We too will go to sea in a Sieve, — To the hills of the Chankly Bore." Far and few, far and few, Are the lands where the Jumblies live; Their heads are green, and their hands are blue, And they went to sea in a Sieve.

From THE JUMBLIES
by Edward Lear

THEY WENT to sea in a Sieve, they did, In a Sieve they went to sea: In spite of all their friends could say, On a winter's morn, on a stormy day, In a Sieve they went to sea! And when the Sieve turned round and round, And every one cried, "You'll all be drowned!" They called aloud, "Our Sieve ain't big, We don't care a button! we don't care a fig! In a Sieve we'll go to sea!" Far and few, far and few, Are the lands where the Jumblies live; Their heads are green, and their hands are blue, And they went to sea in a Sieve.

To fit age 2-3[4-5,6-7,8-9] years, or —
chest 54-56[58-61,63-66,68-71]cm
21-22[23-24,25-26,27-28]in.
Directions for larger sizes are given in square brackets.
Where there is only one set of figures, it applies to all
sizes.

## KNITTED MEASUREMENTS

Underarm (ex. gussets) 66.5[72,77,82.5]cm
26[28,30,32.5]in.
Length 36[40,44,48.5]cm.
Sleeve length 28.5[31,33.5,36]cm.

## MATERIALS

4[4,5,5] Skeins of **Alice Starmore Scottish Fleet** shown
in Coral and Neptune.
1 Set of double-pointed or circular 3mm (US 3) needles.
1 Set of short double-pointed 2.75mm (US 2) needles. 6
Stitch holders. Stitch markers.

## STITCHES

**Stocking Stitch (St.st):** On flat rows k RS rows and p
WS rows. On circular rnds, k every rnd. **Chart Patt:**
Worked in the round above side vents and on sleeves.
Read all rnds from right to left.

## TENSION

30 Sts and 40 rows to 10cm, measured over St.st, using
3mm needles.

## BODY

Back and front lower borders are worked separately,
back and forth in rows, then they are joined into the
round and the body is then worked in one circular piece
to the armhole.
**Lower Border**
With 2 double-pointed or circular 3mm needles, cast on
94[102,110,118] sts. Working back and forth, k 5 rows.
Patt as follows—
**Row 1 (WS):** * P2, k2; rep from * to the last 2 sts; p2.
**Row 2 (RS):** * k2, p2; rep from * to the last 2 sts; k2.
**Row 3 (WS):** K. **Row 4 (RS):** P.
Rep rows 1 through 4 two more times, then work rows 1
& 2 once more (14 rows of patt in total, ending with WS
facing for next row). P 2 rows. Break off yarn and leave
sts on a spare needle.
Work a second identical border, and break off yarn.
**Join Lower Borders**
With double-pointed or circular 3mm needle, cast on 3
sts and mark the first st cast on for beg of rnd and
underarm st; with RS of one border facing k across the
sts and inc 1 st at centre of border; cast on 5 sts and

These fishing shirts have all the practical features
of the traditional fisherman's gansey. They are
made in authentic gansey yarn, worked in the
round, with underarm gussets and sleeves worked
from shoulder to cuff. They are an ideal exercise
for someone starting out in the gansey technique,
for while they possess all the classic features, the
pattern has been kept deliberately simple. Fisher
ganseys were designed for toughness of wear and
ease of movement while working at sea – and are
therefore equally well suited for boys at play, as
shown here by Robert and David.

mark the third st cast on for underarm st; with RS of second border facing k across the sts and inc 1 st at centre of border; cast on 2 sts. 200[216,232,248] Sts. Making sure cast on sts are not twisted, and borders are RS facing, join into a circle and p 1 rnd.

**Next Rnd:** P1 (underarm st); k 99[107,115,123] (front); p1 (underarm st); k 99[107,115,123] (back).

### Set Chart Patt Over Front and Back Sts

**Rnd 1:** * P underarm st; reading from right to left, patt the first 1[2,0,1] sts as indicated; rep the 6 patt sts 16[17,19,20] times; patt the last 2[3,1,2] sts; rep from * once more.

Continue as set, working underarm sts in p throughout, and work through rnd 4 of chart over front and back sts.

**All Foll Rnds:** * P underarm st; k 99[107,115,123]; rep from * once more.

Continue until body measures 14[15.5,18,19]cm from cast on above lower borders.

### Beg Gussets

**Next Rnd** * M1; k underarm st; m1 (these 3 sts beg the gusset - the underarm st becomes the centre st of the gusset); k the next 99[107,115,123] sts; rep from * once more. K 3 rnds.

**Next Rnd:** *M1; k3 (underarm st is at centre); m1; k the next 99[107,115,123] sts; rep from * once more. K 3 rnds.continue as set and inc at each side of gussets on next and every foll 4th rnd until there are 11[13,13,15] sts in each gusset. Break off yarn.

### Divide for Front and Back Yokes

Place the 11[13,13,15] sts of first gusset on a holder; rejoin yarn and k across the 99[107,115,123] sts of front; place the 11[13,13,15] sts of second gusset on a holder; leave the rem sts of back on a spare needle. Turn and continue in St. St. over front sts, working back and forth in rows, until front yoke measures 4[4,5.5,7.5]cm with RS facing for next row.

### Left Front Neck Opening

K 46[50,54,58] sts; cast on 7 sts; leave the rem 53[57,61,65] sts of right side on a spare needle. Turn and work left side of yoke as follows—

**Row 1 (WS):** K2; p2; k3; p 46[50,54,58]. **Row 2 (RS):** K 46[50,54,58]; p1; k1; p1; k2; p1; k1. Rep these 2 rows until front opening measures 4cm from beg, with RS facing for next row.

### Shape Left Side of Neck

**Next Row (RS):**K 42[45,48,51]; place the rem 11[12,13,14] sts on a holder.

+ Turn and continue in St.st and dec 1 st at neck edge of next 6 rows. 36[39,42,45] Sts rem. Work 1 row without shaping then dec 1 st at neck edge of next and every foll alt row 6[7,7,8] times in all. 30[32,35,37] Sts rem.

**Second & Third Sizes Only:** Work 2 more rows in St.st. **All Sizes – Next Row (WS):** Knit. **Next Row (RS):** Knit. Place sts on a holder. ++

### Right Front Neck Opening

With RS facing, rejoin yarn to the 53[57,61,65] sts of right side of front yoke and patt as follows —

**Row 1 (RS):** K1; p1; k2; p1; k1; p1; k 46[50,54,58]. **Row 2 (WS):** P 46[50,54,58]; k3; p2; k2. Rep these 2 rows until front opening matches left opening in length with RS facing for next row. Break off yarn.

### Shape Right Side of Neck

**Next Row (RS):** Place the first 11[12,13,14] sts on a holder; rejoin yarn and k the rem 42[45,48,51] sts. Turn and work as left side from + to ++.

### Back Yoke

With RS facing, rejoin yarn to the 99[107,115,123] sts of back yoke and working back and forth in rows, continue in St.st until back yoke matches front yokes in length to the last 2 rows, with WS facing for next row.

**Next Row (WS):** K 30[32,35,37]; p 39[43,45,49]; k 30[32,35,37].

**Next Row (RS):** Knit.

### Join Front and Back Yokes at Shoulders

Place the 30[32,35,37] sts of left front shoulder on a needle and holding the back yoke needle parallel to the left front needle, use a third needle and cast off the sts of each shoulder together, thus forming a cast off ridge on the RS. Break off yarn and place the next 39[43,45,49] sts of back yoke on a holder for back neck. Place the sts of right front shoulder on a needle. Rejoin yarn and cast off right back and front shoulder sts together as left side.

### Collar

With 3mm needles and RS facing, beg at right side of neck and keeping continuity, patt the first 7 sts from holder as set; k the rem 4[5,6,7] sts from holder; knit up 15[17,17,19] sts evenly along right side of neck; pick up and k the 39[43,45,49] sts from back neck holder; knit up 15[17,17,19] sts evenly along left side of neck; k the first 4[5,6,7] sts from left front holder; keeping continuity, patt the last 7 sts from holder as set. 91[101,105,115] Sts. Patt as follows—

**Row 1 (WS):** K2; p2; k3; * p1, k1: rep from * to the last 8 sts; p1; k3; p2; k2.

**Row 2 (RS):** K1; p1; k2; * p1, k1; rep from * to the last 5 sts; p1; k2; p1; k1.

Rep these 2 rows until k1,p1 rib patt measures 2.5cm with RS facing for next row.

**Third & Fourth Sizes Only:** Patt 2 more rows as set and inc 1 st at centre back neck on last row. 106[116] Sts.

**All Sizes:** Patt as follows—

**Row 1:** K1; p1; * k2; p1; k1; p1; rep from * to the last 4 sts; k2; p1; k1.

**Row 2:** K2; * p2; k3; rep from * to the last 4 sts; p2; k2. Rep these last 2 rows and work 16[18,20,22] rows in total. Cast off loosely and evenly in patt.

## SLEEVES

With set of double-pointed or circular 3mm needles and RS of body facing, pick up and k the 11[13,13,15] sts of gusset and mark the first st for beg of rnd; knit up 79[89,97,109] sts evenly around armhole to complete the rnd. 90[102,110,124] Sts.

### Shape Gusset

Work in St.st and shape gusset as follows—

**Next Rnd:** SSk; k 7[9,9,11]; k2tog; k 79[89,97,109]. K 3 rnds without shaping.

**Next Rnd:** SSk; k 5[7,7,9]; k2tog; k 79[89,97,109]. K 3 rnds without shaping.

Continue as set, decreasing 1 st at each side of gusset on next and every foll 4th rnd until 3 gusset sts rem. K3 rnds without shaping.

**Next Rnd:** Sl2tog knitwise–k1–P2SSO and mark the rem st from this dec to mark beg of rnd and underarm st; k 79[89,97,109] sts.

### Next Rnd – Beg Patt Band

**Rnd 1:** P seam st; beg at rnd 1 of chart and patt the first 0[2,0,0] sts as indicated; rep the 6 patt sts 13[14,16,18] times; patt the last 1[3,1,1] sts as indicated. Continue as set and work through rnd 4.

### Next Rnd – Beg Sleeve Shaping

P underarm st; k2tog; k to the last 2 sts; ssk. 78[88,96,108] Sts rem. P 1 rnd. K 1 rnd (working underarm st in p). P 1 rnd.

**Next Rnd:** P underarm st; k2tog; k to the last 2 sts; ssk. 76[86,94,106] Sts rem.

**Next 2 Rnds:** P seam st; * k2, p2; rep from * to the last 3[1,1,1] sts; k3[1,1,1].

**Next 2 Rnds:** Purl.

Rep these last 4 patt rnds (as lower body borders) and AT THE SAME TIME, keep continuity of patt and dec 1 st at each side of underarm st as set on next and foll 5th rnd. 72[82,90,102] sts rem. Keeping continuity, patt 4 more rnds as set, thus working 14 rnds in total.

**Next Rnd:** P underarm st; k2tog; k to the last 2 sts; ssk. 70[80,88,100] Sts rem.

P1 rnd. K1 rnd (working underarm st in p). P 1 rnd.

**Next Rnd:** P underarm st; k2tog; k to the last 2 sts; ssk. 68[78,86,98] Sts rem.

Set Chart Patt

P seam st; beg at rnd 1 of chart and work the first 0[2,0,0] sts as indicated; rep the 6 patt sts 11[12,14,16] times patt the last 1[3,1,1] sts as indicated. Work through rnd 4 of chart.

Working underarm st in p and all other sts in St.st throughout, dec 1 st at each side of underarm st as set on next and every foll 5th[4th,4th,3rd] rnd until 50[54,56,58] sts rem. Continue straight without shaping until sleeve measures 25[27,29,31]cm from armhole pick up. Change to set of short double-pointed 2.75mm

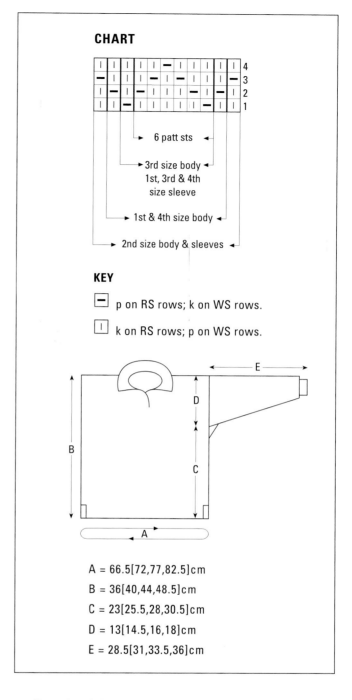

**CHART**

**KEY**

− p on RS rows; k on WS rows.

| k on RS rows; p on WS rows.

A = 66.5[72,77,82.5]cm
B = 36[40,44,48.5]cm
C = 23[25.5,28,30.5]cm
D = 13[14.5,16,18]cm
E = 28.5[31,33.5,36]cm

needles and work k1, p1 rib until sleeve measures 28.5[31,33.5,36]cm. Cast off in rib.

### Side Vent Edges (Work 4)

With 3mm needles and RS facing, knit up 14 sts along end of lower borders. K 2 rows. Cast off knitwise. Sew top end of each edging to cast on sts of body.

### Finishing

Darn in all loose ends. Either rinse in lukewarm water, then spin and dry on a woolly board, or turn WS out and press lightly (omitting ribs), using a warm iron and damp cloth.

The drawing illustrates stitches being knitted up around the armhole. For the sake of clarity, the stitches being knitted up are shown in a contrasting colour, when in fact they will be knitted in the same colour as the garment. The stitches are knitted up by putting the needle through the inside loop of the edge stitch, as shown. You will knit up fewer stitches than there are rows in the armhole, so do not knit up a stitch into every row, but space them as evenly as possible.

The shoulder seam is worked by casting off front and back shoulder stitches together on the right side. This forms a raised seamline, as you can see in the photograph ABOVE. To cast the stitches off together, hold the needles with the front and back shoulder stitches parallel to each other in the left hand. Using a third needle in the right hand, insert it through the first stitch on each needle and knit these stitches

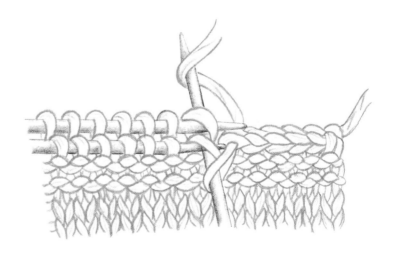

together. Then repeat the process with the next two stitches and cast off the first stitch on the right hand needle. Continue as shown in this drawing until all of the stitches have been cast off together. Make sure that the cast off edge is not too tight. If you find you are making the seam too tight, take it out again and use a larger size of third needle.

# CATS & MICE

Three little mice sat down to spin,
Pussy came by and she looked in.
What are you doing, my fine little men?
We're making coats for gentlemen.
Can I come in and bite off your threads?
Oh no Mistress Pussy!
You'd bite off our heads.

NURSERY RHYME; Traditional

40

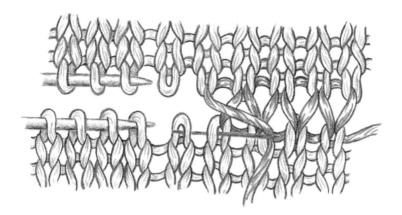

GRAFTING THE SHOULDERS OF CATS & MICE – AN EASY EXAMPLE OF COLOUR KNITTING IN THE ROUND, WORN BY AMY ON THE PREVIOUS PAGE, AND MOLLY OPPOSITE

GRAFTING, also known as Kitchener Stitch, is the method used to join stitches together in order to avoid a seamline. The shoulders of CATS & MICE are grafted. To do this, thread a darning needle in the colour given in the pattern. The thread should be about three times the length of the shoulder seam. Graft together as shown in the drawing, gently pulling the thread as you go along, until the new set of loops formed are equal in size to those of the knitting. They are shown larger in the drawing, simply for the sake of clarity. Darn in both yarn ends on completion.

## SIZES

To fit approx age 2-3[4-5,6-7,8-9] years, or — chest size 54-56[58-61,63-66,68-71]cm 21-22[23-24,25-26,27-28]in.
Directions for larger sizes are given in square brackets. Where there is only one set of figures, it applies to all sizes.

## KNITTED MEASUREMENTS

Underarm 66[72,78,84]cm 26[28.5,31,33]in.
Length 32[37,41,46.5]cm.

## MATERIALS

Of **Alice Starmore Scottish Campion** —
1[2,2,2] Skeins of Mooskit/Shaela.
1 Skein each of Moorit/Eosit, Shaela/White, Mooskit/Black, Thyme, Loganberry, Purple, Aubretia, Violet, Delph, Claret.
1 Set of double-pointed or circular 3.25mm (US 3) needles. 1 Set of short double-pointed 3.25mm (US 3) needles. 4 Stitch holders. Stitch markers.

## STITCHES

**Check Patt:** K2 with first colour, k2 with second colour, stranding the yarns evenly across the WS. Every alt rnd is worked in p. It is important to remember to strand the yarn on the WS after every p2. **Chart Patts:** All rnds are read from right to left. K every rnd, stranding the yarn not in immediate use evenly across the WS. On areas where there are more than 8 sts in one colour, weave in the stranded yarn once at the centre of the stretch. **Steeks:** Worked at armholes and neck and later cut up centre to form openings. Each steek is worked over 8 sts and k on every rnd. On two-colour rnds the steek is worked in alt colours on every st and rnd. Do not weave in newly joined in and broken off yarns at the centre of first armhole steek. Instead leave approx. 5cm tail when joining in and breaking off yarns. **Edge Stitch:** Worked at each side of steeks and k in background colours throughout. Sts for neck and armhole bands are knitted up from edge sts. **Cross Stitch:** With tapestry needle, overcast raw edges of trimmed steeks to strands on WS. After sewing to end reverse to form cross stitches.

## TENSION

30 Sts and 34 rows to 10cm, measured over chart patt using 3.25mm needles. To make an accurate tension swatch, cast on 36 sts on 1 double-pointed or circular needle and rep the 18 patt sts twice. Work as a flat piece, **knitting on the RS only**, and break off the yarns at the end of every row.

## BODY

With 3.25mm needles and Thyme cast on 196[216,232,252] sts. Place a marker at beg of rnd and making sure cast on edge is not twisted, join in and break off colours as required and work 12 rnds of check patt as follows —

**Rnd 1:** * K2 Thyme, k2 Moorit/Eosit; rep from * to end of rnd.

**Rnd 2:** * P2 Thyme, p2 Moorit/Eosit; rep from * to end of rnd.

**Rnds 3 & 4:** As rnds 1 & 2, substituting Moorit/Eosit for Thyme and Loganberry for Moorit/Eosit.

**Rnds 5 & 6:** As set, substituting Purple for Moorit/Eosit and Mooskit/Shaela for Loganberry.

**Rnds 7 & 8:** As set, substituting Mooskit/Shaela for Purple and Aubretia for Mooskit/Shaela.

**Rnds 9 & 10:** As set, substituting Violet for Mooskit/Shaela and Shaela/White for Aubretia.

**Rnds 11 & 12:** As set, substituting Shaela/White for Violet and Delph for Shaela/White. Break off yarns.

### First and Third Sizes – Inc
With Mooskit/Shaela k 49[58]; m1; k 98[116]; m1; k 49[58] (rnd 1 of chart). 198[234] Sts.

### Second and Fourth Sizes
With Mooskit/Shaela k 1 rnd (rnd 1 of chart).

### All Sizes – Set Chart Patt
Beg at rnd 2 of chart and reading from right to left, rep the 18 patt sts 11[12,13,14] times.

Joining in and breaking off colours as required continue as set and rep the 37 patt rnds until 50[62,70,83] rnds have been worked from above check patt border, thus ending on rnd 13[25,33,9] inclusive of chart. Break off yarns.

### Next Rnd – Beg Armhole Shaping
Place the first 6[7,8,9] sts of rnd on a holder; cast on 4 steek sts (with alt colours on sizes working a two-colour rnd) and mark first st cast on for beg of rnd; with background colour cast on 1 edge st; keeping continuity, patt the next 88[95,102,109] sts as set (front); place the next 11[13,15,17] sts on a holder; with background colour cast on 1 edge sts; cast on 8 steek sts as before; with background colour cast on 1 edge st; keeping continuity, patt the next 88[95,102,109] sts as set (back); place the last 5[6,7,8] sts on the first holder; with background colour cast on 1 edge st; cast on 4 steek sts as before.

Keep continuity of patt on front and back sts, and k steek sts in alt colours on two-colour rnds and k edge sts in background colours throughout, dec 1 st at chart patt side of armhole edge sts on the next 3 rnds. 82[89,96,103] Chart patt sts rem on back and front. Patt 1 rnd without shaping, then dec at armholes as set on next and every foll alt rnd 4 times in all. 74[81,88,95] Chart patt sts rem on back and front. Continue as set

without shaping for a further 17[21,24,28] rnds. 79[95,106,123] Rnds worked above check patt border, thus ending on rnd 5[21,32,12] inclusive of chart.

### Next Rnd – Beg Front Neck Shaping
K4 steek sts and k1 edge st as set; patt the next 27[29,32,34] sts as set; place the next 20[23,24,27] sts on a holder; with background colour cast on 1 edge st; cast on 8 steek sts (with alt colours on sizes working a two-colour rnd); with background colour cast on 1 edge st; keeping continuity patt the last 27[29,32,34] sts of front and then work straight as set to end of rnd.

Keeping continuity of patt and working front neck steek and edge sts as armholes, dec 1 st at chart patt side of front neck edge sts on next 6 rnds. 21[23,26,28] Chart patt sts rem on each front shoulder.

Patt 1 rnd without shaping, then dec as set at front neck edge sts on next and every foll alt rnd 3[3,4,5] times in all. 18[20,22,23] Chart patt sts rem on each front shoulder.

### Next Rnd – Beg Back Neck Shaping
Patt straight as set to the 74[81,88,95] sts of back; patt the first 19[21,23,24] sts as set; place the next 36[39,42,47] sts on a holder; with background colour cast on 1 edge st; cast on 8 steek sts (with alt colours on sizes working a two-colour rnd) ; with background colour cast on 1 edge st; keeping continuity patt straight as set to end of rnd.

Keeping continuity of patt and working back neck steek and edge sts as armholes and front, dec 1 st at chart patt side of front and back neck edge sts on next rnd. Dec 1 st at chart patt side of back neck edge sts on next rnd. Dec 1 st as set at front neck edge sts on next rnd. Dec 1 st as set at back neck edge sts on next rnd. 16[18,20,21] Chart patt sts rem on each front and back shoulder. Patt 2[3,3,3] rnds without shaping, casting off all steek sts on last rnd. 99[116,129,148] Rnds worked from above check patt border, thus ending on rnd 25[5,18,37] inclusive of chart.

With Loganberry [Mooskit/Shaela, Mooskit/Shaela, Delph] graft front and back shoulders together including edge sts.

### Armhole Edgings
Cut open armhole steeks up centre, between 4th and 5th steek sts. With RS facing, set of short double-pointed 3.25mm needles and Mooskit/Shaela, beg at centre st of underarm holder and k up sts as follows —
Pick up and k 6[7,8,9] sts from holder, marking first st for beg of rnd; knit up 40[45,50,55] sts evenly to shoulder graft, working into loop of edge st next to chart patt sts; knit up 1 st from shoulder graft; knit up 40[45,50,55] sts evenly to underarm holder, working into edge st as before; pick up and k the rem 5[6,7,8] sts from underarm holder. 92[104,116,128] Sts.

**Rnd 1:** With Mooskit/Shaela knit. **Rnd 2:** With Mooskit/Shaela purl.

# CHART

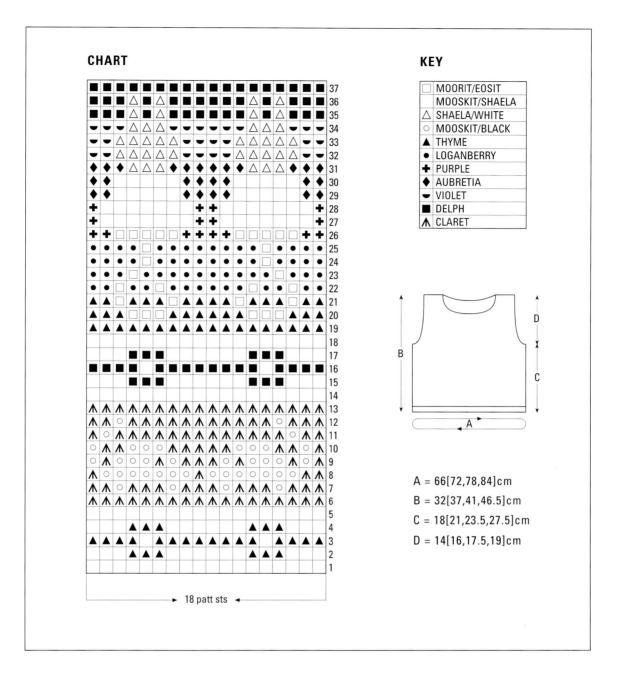

→ 18 patt sts ←

## KEY

| | |
|---|---|
| ☐ | MOORIT/EOSIT |
| | MOOSKIT/SHAELA |
| △ | SHAELA/WHITE |
| ○ | MOOSKIT/BLACK |
| ▲ | THYME |
| ● | LOGANBERRY |
| ✚ | PURPLE |
| ◆ | AUBRETIA |
| ➖ | VIOLET |
| ■ | DELPH |
| ⋀ | CLARET |

A = 66[72,78,84]cm

B = 32[37,41,46.5]cm

C = 18[21,23.5,27.5]cm

D = 14[16,17.5,19]cm

**Rnd 3:** * K1 Delph, k3 Mooskit/Shaela; rep from * to end of rnd.

**Rnd 4:** * P1 Delph, p3 Mooskit/Shaela; rep from * to end of rnd.

**Rnds 5 & 6:** As rnds 1 & 2.

With Mooskit/Shaela cast off knitwise.

### Neckband

Cut open back and front neck steek sts up centre between 4th and 5th steek sts. With RS facing, set of short double-pointed 3.25mm needles and Mooskit/Shaela, beg at back neck holder and knit up sts as follows —

Pick up and k the 36[39,42,47] sts from back neck holder, marking first st for beg of rnd; knit up 20[21,23,25] sts evenly along left side of neck working into loop of edge st next to chart patt sts; pick up and k the 20[23,24,27] sts from front neck holder; knit up 20[21,23,25] sts evenly along right side of neck, working into edge sts as before. 96[104,112,124] Sts.

Work 6 rnds as armhole edgings. With Mooskit/Shaela cast off knitwise.

### FINISHING

Trim all steeks to a 2 stitch width and with Mooskit/Shaela, cross stitch steeks in position. Darn in loose ends. Using a warm iron and damp cloth, press garment very lightly on WS, omitting check patt border, neckband and armhole edgings.

# MAGIC CARPET

They say it came from Samarkand
By Caravanserai,
Then found its way to fair England,
Though none can tell just how or why,
Since no-one knows its history,
It really is a mystery:
But soon I'll find its secret,
For I'm certain it can fly.

I see it in the parlour where
I'm not supposed to play,
But sometimes I will creep in there
To marvel at its bright array,
Its silken colours blazing
And its birds and beasts amazing,
Though whether real or fable
I most surely cannot say.

When I unlock its secret then
I'll travel far and wide,
With just my faithful dog, Old Ben,
Full fearlessly we'll soar and glide,
'Cross wild Caucasian mountains
And exotic eastern fountains,
To see Kings and Maharajahs
Dwelling on the other side.

We'll see the mosques of Baghdad
And the sands of Arabie;
Then pay respects to Sinbad
In his ship upon the warm Red Sea;
We'll view Constantinople
With its spires of jade and opal,
Then we'll fly along the rainbow
To be home in time for tea.

From THE MAGIC CARPET
by Algernon Dashwood

46

The 'birds and beasts amazing' on this intarsia sweater come from Caucasian carpets. There is also some stranded knitting in the horizontal band on the lower body. For technical and aesthetic reasons of size and scale, this band is slightly different for each of the four sizes. You will find this explained in the pattern. Sam is shown here wearing the third size. The pattern calls for little touches of nine different colours, so this is an ideal opportunity to use any suitable oddments of yarn in order to knit your own special MAGIC CARPET.

To fit age 2-3[4-5,6-7,8-9] years or —
chest 54-56[58-61,63-66,68-71]cm
21-22[23-24,25-26,27-28]in.
Directions for larger sizes are given in square brackets.
Where there is only one set of figures, it applies to all sizes.

## KNITTED MEASUREMENTS

Underarm 73[79,85,91]cm 28.5[31,33.5,36]in.
Length 35[40,45,49]cm.
Sleeve length 24[27,30,33]cm.

## MATERIALS

Of **Alice Starmore Bainin**—
3[3,3,4] Skeins of Mulberry.
Oddments of 9 contrasting colours. The yarns and colours used here are as follows—
Of **Alice Starmore Bainin**—
Brick and Ruby.
Of **Alice Starmore Scottish Heather**—
Mooskit, Autumn, Lichen, Burnt Umber, Hydrangea, Amethyst and Wilde Mushroom.
1 Pair 4.5mm (US 7) needles. 2 Stitch Holders.

## STITCHES

**Main Chart Patts:** Worked entirely in St. st (k RS rows, p WS rows). Odd numbered rows are RS and are worked from right to left. Even numbered rows are WS and are worked from left to right. Use separate lengths of yarn for each area of colour. Link one colour to the next on every row by crossing the yarn from the last colour worked **over** the yarn for the next colour before working the next st. **Border Charts:** Worked using both stranding and separate lengths of yarn. Each size has a different number of border rows and RS and WS rows are worked according to each size.

## TENSION

20 Sts and 26 rows, measured over main chart patt using 4.5mm needles.

## BACK

* With 4.5mm needles and Mulberry, cast on 70[74,82,86] sts. K 2 rows. Join in Autumn and stranding the yarns across the WS, patt as follows—
**Row 1 (RS):** * K2 Autumn, k2 Mulberry; rep from * to the last 2 sts; K2 Autumn.
**Row 2 (WS):** As row 1, but bring yarn forward for stranding on the WS after every k2.
Break off Autumn and with Mulberry k 2 rows. Join in Brick and stranding the yarns across the WS as set on rows 1 & 2, patt 2 rows as follows—

* K2 Mulberry, k2 Brick; rep from * to the last 2 sts; k2 Mulberry.
Break off Brick and with Mulberry k 2 rows. Join in Autumn and work 2 rows as row 1 & 2. Break off Autumn and with Mulberry k 2 rows. **

**First and Third Sizes Only**
With Mulberry, k 1 row.
**Next Row (WS) – Inc:** P1; (m1, p 34[40]) twice; m1; p1. 73[85] Sts.
**Second and Fourth Sizes Only**
**Next Row (RS) – Inc**
K1; (m1, k 18[21]) 4 times; m1; k1. 79[91] Sts.
Working all RS rows in k and all WS rows in p, work the border patt chart(s) as follows—
**First Size**
Using a separate length of yarn for each area of colour, and stranding the Mulberry yarn across the WS, beg with a RS row and patt the 11 rows of chart B. With Mulberry, p 1 WS row.
**Second Size**
With Lichen and Burnt Umber, beg with a WS row and stranding the colours across the WS, patt the first 3 rows of chart A, repeating the 6 patt sts 13 times and work the first st on WS rows and the last st on RS rows, as indicated. Break off yarns. Using a separate yarn for each area of colour, and stranding the Mulberry yarn across the WS, patt the 11 rows of chart B. With Lichen and Burnt Umber work the first 3 rows of chart A as before. Break off yarns.
**Third Size**
Joining in and breaking off colours as required, strand the colours across the WS and beg with a RS row, work the first 6 rows of chart A, repeating the 6 patt sts 14 times and working the last st on RS rows and the first st on WS rows, as indicated. Break off yarns. using a separate length of yarn for each area of colour, and stranding the Mulberry yarn across the WS, patt the 11 rows of chart B. Joining in and breaking off colours as required, beg at row 4 (WS) of chart A and stranding the yarns across the WS, patt through row 9 of chart A. Break off yarns. With Mulberry, p 1 WS row.
**Fourth Size**
Joining in and breaking off colours as required, beg with a WS row and stranding the colours across the WS, patt the 9 rows of chart A, repeating the 6 patt sts 15 times and working the first st on WS rows and the last st on RS rows, as indicated. Using a separate length of yarn for each area of colour, and stranding the Mulberry yarn across the WS, patt the 11 rows of chart B. Joining and breaking off colours as required work the 9 rows of chart A as before. Break off yarns.
**All Sizes**
With RS facing, beg at row 1 of chart C and reading all RS rows from right to left and all WS rows from left to

right, use a separate length of yarn for each area of colour and work the 66[72,78,84] rows over the 73[79,85,91] sts as outlined on chart.

**Next Row (RS):** With Mulberry cast off 22[24,26,28] sts; k the next 29[31,33,35] sts and place these sts on a holder; cast off the rem 22[24,26,28] sts.

## FRONT

As back through row 53[57,61,65] of chart C thus ending with WS facing for next row.

**Shape Neck**

Working row 54[58,62,66] of chart, patt the first 28[31,34,37] sts as indicated; place the next 17 sts on a holder; leave the rem 28[31,34,37] sts on a spare needle. Shape right side of neck as follows—

+ Turn and continue working from chart and dec 1 st at neck edge on next 2 rows as indicated, then dec 1st at neck edge of every foll alt row 4[5,6,7] times as indicated. 22[24,26,28] Sts rem. Patt straight through row 66[72,82,92]. With Mulberry cast off shoulder sts.
++

With WS facing rejoin yarn to the 28[31,34,37] sts of left side of neck and work row 54[58,62,66] as indicated. Continue working chart and shape neck as left side from + to ++.

## SLEEVES

With 4.5mm needles and Mulberry, cast on 30[34,38,42] sts. Work 14 rows as back from * to **. K 1 row.

**Next Row (WS) – Inc**

With Mulberry, p 3[2,1,3]; * m1; p 4[5,6,6]; rep from * 6 times in all; m1; p 3[2,1,3]. 37[41,45,49] Sts.

Using a separate length of yarn for each area of colour, beg at row 1 of chart D and reading all RS rows from right to left and all WS rows from left to right, work the patt as indicated, increasing 1 st at each side of 3rd and every foll 3rd row 8[6,6,6] times in all, then continue to inc as indicated on every foll 4th row 5[8,10,12] times in all. 63[69,77,85] Sts. Patt a further 7 rows as indicated, thus ending on row 51[57,65,73] inclusive. With Mulberry, cast off all sts purlwise.

## FINISHING

Darn in all loose ends. Press pieces lightly on WS, using a warm iron and a damp cloth, omitting textured borders. With Mulberry, sew back and front together at left shoulder seam.

**Neckband**

With RS facing, 4.5mm needles and Mulberry, pick up and k the 29[31,33,35] sts from back neck holder; knit up 12[13,14,15] sts along left side of neck; pick up and k the 17 sts from front neck holder; knit up 12[13,14,15] sts along right side of neck. 70[74,78,82] Sts. Patt as follows—

With Mulberry, k 3 rows. Join in Brick and patt the next 2 rows as follows—

* K2 mulberry, k2 Brick ; rep from *, stranding the colours on the WS. Break off Brick.

With Mulberry k 3 rows.

With WS facing, cast off knitwise.

Darn in loose neckband ends, sew up neckband and right shoulder seam. Press shoulder seams lightly on WS using a warm iron and damp cloth. Place centre top of sleeves at shoulder seams and sew sleeves to body. Press seams lightly on WS as before. Sew up side and sleeve seams and press seams lightly on WS as before.

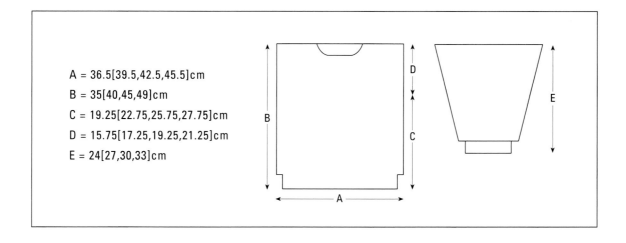

A = 36.5[39.5,42.5,45.5]cm

B = 35[40,45,49]cm

C = 19.25[22.75,25.75,27.75]cm

D = 15.75[17.25,19.25,21.25]cm

E = 24[27,30,33]cm

**CHART C**

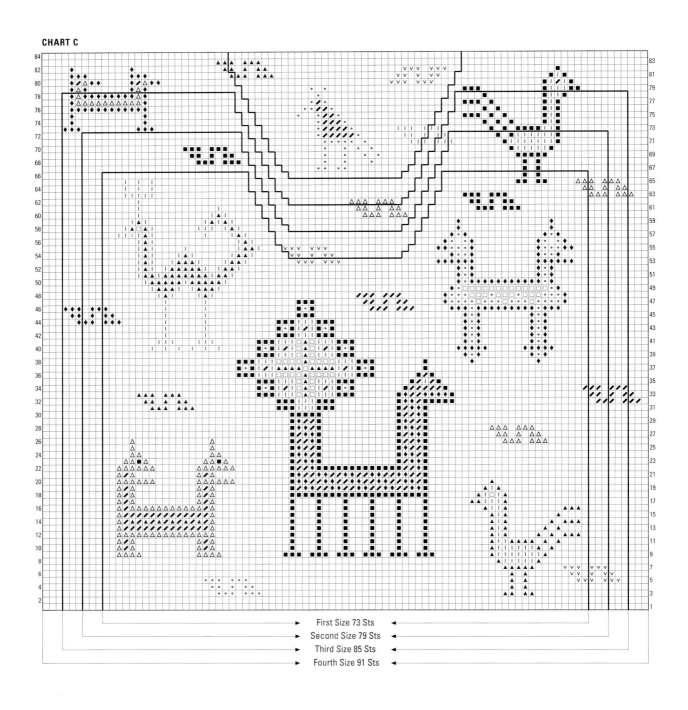

First Size 73 Sts
Second Size 79 Sts
Third Size 85 Sts
Fourth Size 91 Sts

**CHART B**

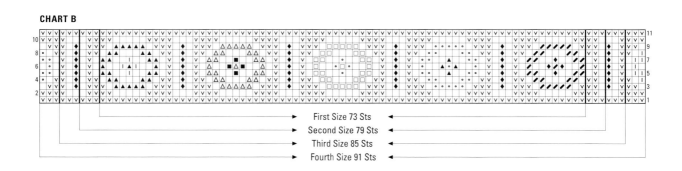

First Size 73 Sts
Second Size 79 Sts
Third Size 85 Sts
Fourth Size 91 Sts

**CHART D**

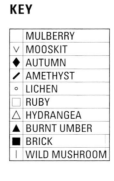
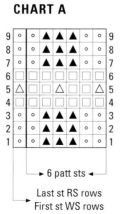

First Size 37 Sts
Second Size 41 Sts
Third Size 45 Sts
Fourth Size 49 Sts

**CHART A**

6 patt sts

Last st RS rows
First st WS rows

**KEY**

| | |
|---|---|
| | MULBERRY |
| ∨ | MOOSKIT |
| ◆ | AUTUMN |
| ╱ | AMETHYST |
| ○ | LICHEN |
| ☐ | RUBY |
| △ | HYDRANGEA |
| ▲ | BURNT UMBER |
| ■ | BRICK |
| I | WILD MUSHROOM |

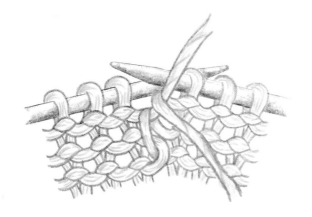

LINKING COLOURS.

When using separate lengths of yarn for each area of colour, it is important to link one colour to the next in order to avoid gaps in the knitting. The drawing AT LEFT shows how to link one colour to the next by simply crossing the yarn from the colour just worked, OVER the yarn about to be worked.

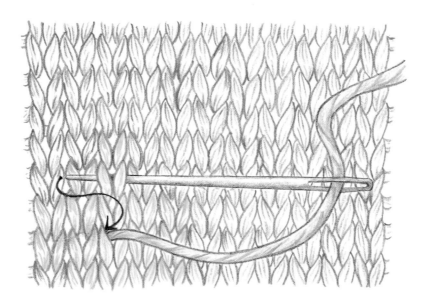

DUPLICATE STITCH. In tiny areas of the pattern – such as the eyes of the creatures and other small details – you may prefer to duplicate stitch the colour in afterwards instead of knitting it in at the time. For example, I found it easier to duplicate stitch the coloured diamond at the centre of each lozenge on Chart B. The drawing above shows an eye being duplicate stitched. Thread a tapestry needle with the appropriate colour and bring it through the work, from the back so that it comes out on the right side, at the BASE of the stitch to be covered. Then insert the needle from right to left, under the two threads of the stitch immediately above, as shown. Then take it through to the wrong side at the base of the stitch being covered, as indicated by the arrow above. Darn in the ends on the wrong side. If more than one stitch is being covered, then bring out the needle at the base of the next required stitch and repeat the process.

Thomas is wearing his MAGIC CARPET in the first size for age 2 to 3 years.
Note that the horizontal band for this size is composed of Chart B only.

# SAND DOLLAR

"Will you walk a little faster?" said a whiting to a snail,
"There's a porpoise close behind us, and he's treading on my tail.
See how eagerly the lobsters and the turtles all advance!
They are waiting on the shingle – will you come and join the dance?
Will you, won't you, will you, won't you, will you join the dance?
Will you, won't you, will you, won't you, won't you join the dance?

"You really have no notion how delightful it will be
When they take us up and throw us, with the lobsters, out to sea!"
But the snail replied "Too far, too far!" and gave a look askance –
Said he thanked the whiting kindly, but he would not join the dance.
Would not, could not, would not, could not, would not join the dance.
Would not, could not, would not, could not, could not join the dance.

"What matters it how far we go?" his scaly friend replied.
"There is another shore, you know, upon the other side.
The further off from England the nearer is to France –
Then turn not pale, beloved snail, but come and join the dance.
Will you, won't you, will you, won't you, will you join the dance?
Will you, won't you, will you, won't you, won't you join the dance?"

From ALICE'S ADVENTURES IN WONDERLAND by Lewis Carroll

56

To fit age 6-7[8-9] years, or —
chest 63-66[68-71]cm 25-26[27-28]in.
Directions for larger sizes are given in square brackets.
Where there is only one set of figures, it applies to both sizes.

## KNITTED MEASUREMENTS

Underarm (ex. gussets) 70[78]cm 27.5[31]in.
Length 55[61]cm. Sleeve length 30[32]cm.

## MATERIALS

10[12] Balls of **Alice Starmore Scottish Fleet** shown in Sea Green.
1 Set of double-pointed or circular 3mm (US 3) needles.
1 Set of short double-pointed 3mm needles to work the shoulder join and lower sleeves.
1 Set of double-pointed or short circular 2.75mm (US 2) needles.
1 Cable needle. 6 Stitch holders. Stitch markers.

## STITCHES

**Chart Patts:** On areas worked in the round, all charts are read from right to left. On areas worked back and forth in rows, all RS rows are read from right to left and all WS rows are read from left to right. **Note:** On charts A through E, all make ones' (M) are worked by picking up the strand running between the last stitch worked and the next st to be worked, and knitting into the back of the strand. On underarm gussets, all make ones' (M) are worked by picking up the loop of the stitch below the next st to be worked and k into the loop. See pages XXX.

## TENSION

28 Sts and 40 rows to 10cm, measured over chart G patt, using 3mm needles. To make a swatch, cast on 40 sts and rep the 10 patt sts 4 times.

## BODY

With set of double-pointed or circular 3mm needles, cast on 336[392]sts. Place a marker at beg of rnd, and making sure cast on edge is not twisted, k1 rnd, then p 1 rnd.
Beg at rnd 1 of chart A and rep the 28 patt sts 12[14] times in the rnd. Continue as set and rep the 12 patt rnds of chart A 2[3] times in all (24[36] rnds).
Work rnd 1 of chart B repeating the 26 patt sts 12[14] times in the rnd. 312[364] Sts rem. Continue as set and work through rnd 12 of chart. Rep the 12 patt rnds 1 more time (24 rnds chart B in total), but on these reps, work M1 instead of first and last k sts on row 1, as indicated on chart, so that the stitch count remains the same throughout all rnds of chart B.
Beg at rnd 1 of chart C repeating the 24 patt sts 12[14]

times in the rnd. 288[336] Sts rem. Continue as set and work through rnd 12 of chart. Rep the 12 patt rnds 1 more time (24 rnds chart C in total), but on these reps work M1 on row 1, as indicated on chart, thus keeping the st count the same throughout.
Beg at rnd 1 of chart D repeating the 22 patt sts 12[14] times in the rnd. 264[308] Sts rem. Continue as set and work through rnd 12 of chart. Rep the 12 patt rnds once more (24 rnds chart D in total), but on second rep, work M1 on row 1 as indicated on chart, thus keeping the stitch count the same throughout.
Beg at rnd 1 of chart E repeating the 20 patt sts 12[14] times in the rnd. 240[280] Sts rem. Continue as set and work through rnd 11. 216[252] Sts rem. Work rnd 12 of chart E.

### Next Rnd – Dec and Mark Gusset Sts
**First Size:** * K1 and mark this st for gusset; k1; (k2tog, k4) 17 times; k2tog; k2; rep from * once more. 180 Sts rem.
**Second Size:** * K1 and mark this st for gusset; k1; (k2tog, k3) 6 times; (k2tog, k2) 16 times; (k2tog, k3) 6 times; rep from * once more. 196 Sts rem.

### Both Sizes – Beg Gussets
**Next Rnd:** Working all incs into loop below next st, m1; k1; m1 (these 3 sts form the first gusset); p 89[97] sts (back); m1; k1; m1 (these 3 sts form the second gusset); p 89[97] sts (front).
**Next Rnd:** * K3 gusset sts; p 89[97] sts; rep from * once more.
**Next Rnd:** Knit.

### Next Rnd – Set Chart F Patt over Back and Front Sts
* K3 (gusset); beg at rnd 1 of chart F and patt the first 4 sts as indicated; rep the 8 patt sts (inc as indicated); 10[11] times; patt the last 5 sts as indicated. 111[121] chart F sts; rep from * once more.
Continue as set, working all gusset sts in k throughout and inc 1 st at each side of gusset on next and every foll 4th rnd, and AT THE SAME TIME work the 20 rnds of chart F on back and front sts as set, decreasing on rnd 20 as indicated on chart. 89[97] Sts rem on each of back and front and 13 sts in each gusset.
**Next Rnd:** Knit.
**Next Rnd:** * M1; k13; m1; p 89[97]; rep from * once more.
**Next Rnd:** * K15; p 89[97]; rep from * once more.

### Divide for Back and Front Yokes
* K the 15 gusset sts and place these sts on a holder; inc over the next 89[97] sts as follows—
K2; (m1, k4) 21[23] times; m1; k3 – 111[121]sts; rep from * once more. Break off yarn and place the last 111[121] sts (front) on a spare needle.

### Back Yoke
+ With RS facing and working back and forth in rows, beg at row 1 of charts and set the yoke patt over the 111[121] sts of back as follows—

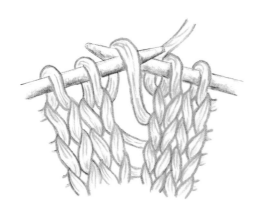

### DRAWING 1: M BETWEEN STITCHES

This is the method used to make a stitch (M) on Charts A through E. To make this increase, insert the left needle point from front to back, under the strand that runs between the two needles: knit into the back of the strand as shown. The strand will cross at the base when the new stitch is made.

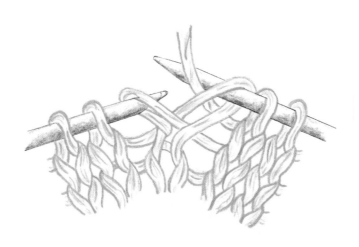

### DRAWING 2: THE LIFTED INCREASE

This is the method used to increase a stitch (M) at each side of the underarm gussets. Insert the right needle point through the front of the loop below the next stitch, as shown: then knit into this loop to form the new stitch.

### DRAWING 3: PURL 3 TOGETHER (P3TOG)

This decrease is used at the centre of each pattern panel on Charts A through E. Insert the right needle through the fronts of the next 3 stitches, as shown, and purl to form 1 stitch. It is important to exert a little extra tension on the new stitch to prevent the weight of the 3 stitches from stretching it.

**Row 1 (RS):** Reading from right to left, beg on 7th[2nd] st and patt the last 4[9] sts of chart G then rep the 10 patt sts 3 times; work chart H over the next 43 sts; rep the 10 patt sts of chart J 3 times, then patt the first 4[9] sts.

**Row 2 (WS):** Reading from left to right, patt the last 4[9] sts of chart J, then rep the 10 patt sts 3 times; work chart H over the next 43 sts; rep the 10 patt sts of chart G 3 times then patt the first 4[9] sts.

Continue as set and rep the 10 patt rows of charts G and J and work through row 10 of chart H once and thereafter, rep rows 11 – 26 (inc 2 sts on row 13 and dec 2 sts on row 23, as indicated). ++

Work 62[68] patt rows in total, thus ending after working row 2[8] of charts G and J, and row 14[20] of chart H.

### Shape Back Neck

**Next Row (RS):** K 29[33] sts; place the next 55[57] sts on a holder; leave the rem 29[33] sts on a spare needle. Turn and shape right shoulder as follows—

**Next Row (WS):** K2tog; k to end of row. 28[32] Sts rem. P 2 rows. Place sts on a holder.

With RS facing rejoin yarn to the 29[33]sts on spare needle and k to end of row. Shape left shoulder as follows—

**Next Row (WS):** K to the last 2 sts; k2tog. 28[32] Sts rem. P 2 rows. Place sts on a holder.

### Front Yoke

Work as back yoke from + to ++. Work 48[52] patt rows in total, thus ending after working row 8[2] of charts G and J, and row 16[20] of chart H.

### Shape Front Neck

**Next Row (RS):** Keeping continuity, patt the 34[39] sts of chart G; patt the first st of chart H; place the next 43 sts of chart H on a holder; leave the rem 35[40] sts on a spare needle. Turn and shape left side of neck as follows—

+ Keeping continuity of patt, dec 1 st at neck edge of the next 2 rows, then on every foll alt row 5[6] times. 28[32] Sts rem. Patt 1 row without shaping, thus ending with RS facing for next row. K 2 rows. P 2 rows. Place sts on a holder. ++

With RS facing rejoin yarn to the 35[40] sts of right side, and keeping continuity of chart J, patt to end of row. Shape right side as left, from + to ++.

### Join Shoulders

Turn body inside out (shoulders are joined on WS). Place front and back sts of one shoulder on two separate double-pointed 3mm needles. Hold the needles with shoulder sts parallel, with RS of yokes together, and with a third 3mm needle beg at armhole edge and cast off sts together, working to neck edge. Break off yarn and fasten off.

With RS facing and 3mm needles, k the 15 sts from gusset holder; knit up 93[101] sts evenly around armhole to complete the rnd.

### Shape Gussets and Set Sleeve Patt

Place a marker on right hand needle to mark beg of rnd.

**Next Rnd:** Ssk; k11; k2tog (gusset); beg at rnd 1 of chart G and reading from right to left, patt the last 2[1] sts; rep the 10 patt sts 9[10] times, then patt the first 1[0] sts.

Continue working chart G over sleeve sts as set, and working all gusset sts in k throughout, dec 1 st at each side of gusset as set, on every foll 4th rnd until 3 gusset sts rem. Work 3 rnds as set, without shaping.

**Next Rnd:** Sl1-k2tog-psso (1 gusset st rem); continue in patt as set to end of rnd. 94[102] Sts rem.

**Next Rnd:** P1 and mark this st for seam st and beg of rnd; continue in patt as set to end of rnd.

**Next 3 Rnds:** P seam st; continue in patt as set to end of rnd.

**Next Rnd:** P seam st; k2tog; keeping continuity, patt as set to the last 2 sts; ssk.

Rep these last 4 rnds until 50[52] sts rem. Continue straight as set until sleeve measures 29[31]cm from pick-up line.

### Next Rnd – Dec

**First Size:** K2;( k2tog, k10) 4 times. 46 Sts rem.
**Second Size:** (K2tog, k11) 4 times. 48 Sts rem.
**Both Sizes:** K 1 rnd. P 3 rnds. Cast off purlwise.

### Neckband

With RS facing and set of double-pointed or circular 2.75mm needles, beg at back neck holder and pick up and k the 55[57] sts from holder and dec 6 sts evenly over chart H patt – 49[51]sts rem from holder; knit up 17[18] sts sts evenly along left neck edge; pick up and k the 43 sts from front neck holder and dec 6 sts evenly – 37 sts rem from holder; knit up 17[18] sts evenly along right neck edge to complete the rnd. 120[124] Sts.

Place a marker at beg of rnd and p 3 rnds. K 1 rnd.

### Next Rnd – Dec

K 8[12]; * k2tog, k12; rep from * to end of rnd. 112[116] Sts rem.

P 3 rnds. K 2 rnds. P 2 rnds. Cast off purlwise.

FINISHING

Darn in all loose ends. Rinse in lukewarm water. Spin and lay out garment on towels on a flat surface, away from direct heat/sunlight. Smooth out to measurements given on schematic, using pins to anchor the pointed ends of the hemline. Leave in position to dry completely.

## CHART A

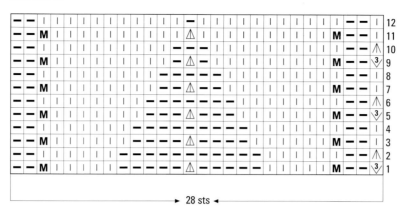

→ 28 sts ←

## CHART B

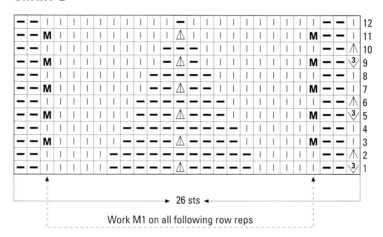

→ 26 sts ←

Work M1 on all following row reps

## CHART C

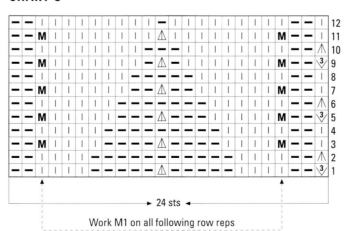

→ 24 sts ←

Work M1 on all following row reps

## CHART D

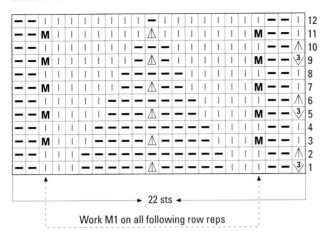

→ 22 sts ←

Work M1 on all following row reps

## CHART E

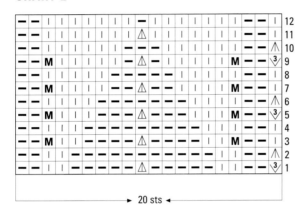

→ 20 sts ←

## CHART F

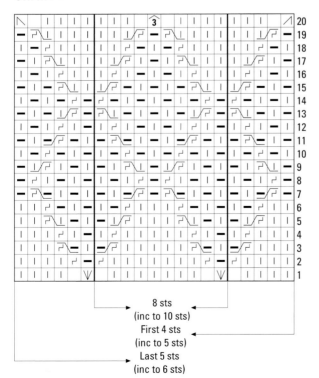

8 sts
(inc to 10 sts)

First 4 sts
(inc to 5 sts)

Last 5 sts
(inc to 6 sts)

## KEY

▬ p on RS rows; k on WS rows.

❘ k on RS rows; p on WS rows.

⌐ k into back of st on RS rows; p into back of st on WS rows.

⦦3 k1, p1, k1 into SAME st, thus making 3 sts from 1.

△ p3tog.

◬ sl 2 sts tog knitwise; k1; pass the 2 slipped sts over the k st.

**M** make 1 st by picking up the strand between the last st worked and the next st, and k into the back of strand.

◲ sl first st to cn and hold at back; k into back of next st; p1 from cn.

◱ sl first st to cn and hold at front; p1; k into back of st from cn.

◲ sl first st to cn and hold at back; k1b; k1 from cn.

◱ sl first st to cn and hold at front; k1; k1b from cn.

◲ sl first st to cn and hold at back; k2b; p1 from cn.

◱ sl first 2 sts to cn and hold at front; p1; k2b from cn.

Ⅴ (k1b, k1) into same st, then insert left hand needle point between the vertical strand that runs down between the 2 sts just made and k into this strand, making the third st of the group.

⦣3 sl 2 sts knitwise, one at a time, with yarn at back, drop yarn, then pass the second st on right needle over first (centre st): sl centre st back to left needle and pass next st on left needle over it: k the rem centre st.

◲ sl first st to cn and hold at back; k2b; then k1b from cn.

◱ sl first 2 sts to cn and hold at front; k1b; then k2b from cn.

◱ sl first 2 sts to cn and hold at front; k1; k2b from cn.

◲ sl first st to cn and hold at back; k2b; k1 from cn.

☐ no stitch.

**CHART H**

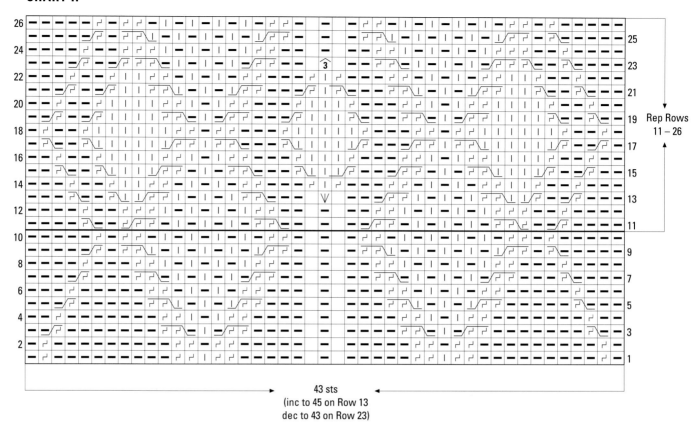

Rep Rows
11 – 26

43 sts
(inc to 45 on Row 13
dec to 43 on Row 23)

**CHART G**

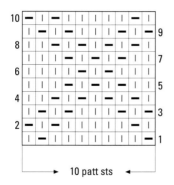

10 patt sts

**CHART J**

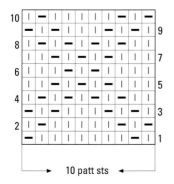

10 patt sts

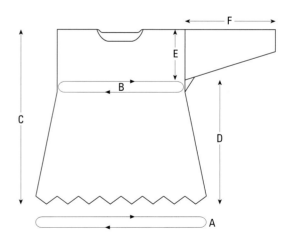

A = 96[112]cm

B = 70[78]cm

C = 55[61]cm

D = 38.5[43]cm

E = 16.5[18]cm

F = 30[32]cm

SAND DOLLAR, worn here by Laurie, first appeared as a woman's design, and became popular with knitters of above average ability. Due to many requests, it has been recalculated as a special design for girls aged 6 to 9 years. It is still intended to be a design for skilled knitters. It does not allow for imperfect tension. The effort is worthwhile, for despite its exquisitely intricate appearance, it is made of gansey yarn and if looked after correctly, will survive to be passed down the generations.

# ELEPHANTS

DO ELEPHANTS PASS BY THIS WAY ?
He asked of me just yesterday,
Just yesterday, while hard at play
In gentle summer weather.
Our cool and rainy British Isles,
Are north of India by miles,
And so I covered up my smiles
And answered – dear, no never.

The sadness on his features chaste
Made me regret my undue haste;
I looked upon his boyish face,
So recently a baby.
Emotion with cold logic fought,
This cruel dilemma had me caught,
I cast aside all I'd been taught
And swiftly said – well, maybe.

If when the dark of night is done,
And misty dawn has just begun
And over there the morning sun
Is in the west arising,
Then it's a certain fact my dear
That elephants may well appear,
And you may see them large and clear
With other things surprising.

The honeysuckle scents the breeze,
I see him crouched upon his knees
Down in amongst the garden trees,
Where lazy cats are sunning.
I see him jump, I hear his cry,
He comes to me with arms held high.
Across the lawn to where I lie,
At full tilt he is running.

Elephants on jungle trail!
He gasps, I saw them trunk to tail,
They swayed like ships in fullest sail,
Their Mahouts loudly singing.
And on the largest in the line,
Upon his back, a howdah fine,
With rich red jewels like ruby wine
And golden bells all ringing.

Philosophers would smile and say,
The sun rose in the west today
If he saw such a rare display,
For surely he's romancing.
I care not for the worldly-wise,
I think that life can still surprise,
For in the bright orbs of his eyes
The elephants were dancing.

From ELEPHANTS by Celia Devenish

## SIZES

To fit approx age 2-3[4-5,6-7,8-9] years, or — chest 54-56[58-61,63-66, 68-71]cm 21-22[23-24,25-26,27-28]in.

Directions for larger sizes are given in square brackets. Where there is only one set of figures, it applies to all sizes.

## KNITTED MEASUREMENTS

Underarm (buttoned) 68[73,78,82]cm 27[29,31,32.25]in.

Length 33[37,41,45]cm.

## MATERIALS

Of **Alice Starmore Scottish Campion**—
1[2,2,2] Skeins each of Dark Green, Bronze and Cobalt.
1[1,2,2] Skeins each of Burnt Umber, Ink and Ginger.
1 Skein of Violet.
1 Set of double-pointed or circular 3.25mm (US 3) needles. 1 Set of short double-pointed 3.25mm (US 3) needles.
3 Stitch holders. Stitch markers. 6[6,7,7] Buttons.

## STITCHES

**Border Patt:** Work as directed and on two-colour rnds/rows, strand the yarns evenly across the WS. On flat rows every row is worked in k, and on circular rnds every alt rnd is worked in p. It is important to remember to strand the yarn on the WS after working the colours in p. **Chart Patt:** All rnds are read from right to left. K every rnd, stranding the yarn not in immediate use evenly across the WS. **Steeks:** Worked at front, armholes and neck and later cut up centre to form openings. Each steek is worked over 8 sts and k on every rnd. On two-colour rnds, the steek sts are worked in alt colours on every st and rnd. Do not weave in newly joined in or broken off yarns at centre of front steek. Instead leave approx 5cm tail when joining in and breaking off yarns. **Edge Stitch:** Worked at each side of steeks and k in background colours throughout. Sts for front and armhole bands are knitted up from edge st. **Cross Stitch:** With tapestry needle, overcast raw edges of trimmed steeks to strands on WS, and after sewing to end, reverse to form cross stitches.

## TENSION

30 Sts and 34 rows to 10cm, measured over chart patt using 3.25mm needles. To make an accurate tension swatch, cast on 36 sts on 1 double-pointed or circular needle and patt the last 4 sts of rep; patt the 28 sts and then patt the first 4 sts. Work a flat piece, **knitting on the RS only**, breaking off the yarns at the end of every row.

## BODY

With 3.25mm needles and Dark Green, cast on 195[211,223,235] sts. Place a marker at beg of rnd and making sure cast on edge is not twisted, join in and break off colours as required and set the front steek, edge sts and border patt as follows—

**Rnd 1:** With alt Burnt Umber and Dark Green k4 steek sts; with Dark Green, k1 edge st; * k1 Burnt Umber, k1 Dark Green; rep from * to the last 6 sts; k1 Burnt Umber; with Dark Green k1 edge st; with alt colours k4 steek sts.

**Rnd 2:** With alt colours k4 steek sts; with Dark Green k1 edge st; * p1 Burnt Umber, p1 Dark Green; rep from * to the last 6 sts; p1 Burnt Umber; with Dark Green k1 edge st; with alt colours, k4 steek sts.

**Rnd 3:** With Burnt Umber, k.

**Rnd 4:** With Burnt Umber, k5; p to the last 5 sts; k5.

**Rnd 5:** With alt Ink and Bronze k4 steek sts; with Ink k1 edge st; * k1 Bronze, k3 Ink; rep from * to the last 6 sts; k1 Bronze; with Ink k1 edge st; with alt colours k4 steek sts.

**Rnd 6:** With alt colours k4 steek sts; with Ink k1 edge st; * p1 Bronze, p3 Ink; rep from * to the last 6 sts; p1 Bronze; with Ink k1 edge st; with alt colours k4 steek sts.

**Rnds 7 & 8:** As rnds 5 & 6, substituting Cobalt for Ink. Break off yarns.

**Next Rnd – Inc**

With Dark Green, k 9[6,7,7]; * m1, k 16[22,19,17]; rep from * to the last 10[7,7,7] sts; m1; k 10[7,7,7]. 207[221,235,249] Sts (this rnd counts as rnd 1 of chart patt).

**Next Rnd – Beg Chart Patt**

Join in Burnt Umber and reading all rnds from right to left, set the patt as follows—

**First & Third Sizes:** With alt colours, k4 steek sts; with Dark Green k1 edge st; beg at rnd 2 and rep the 28 patt sts 7[8] times; patt first st of chart; with Dark Green k1 edge st; with alt colours k4 steek sts.

**Second & Fourth Sizes:** With alt colours k4 steek sts; with Dark Green k1 edge st; beg at rnd 2 and patt the last 8 sts of chart; rep the 28 patt 7[8] times; patt the first 7 sts of chart; with Dark Green k1 edge st; with alt colours k4 steek sts.

Joining in and breaking off colours as required, continue as set, working edge sts in background colours through-out, and steek sts in alt colours on two-colour rnds. Rep the 28 patt rnds and work 57[66,74,84] patt rnds in total, thus ending on rnd 1[10,18,28] inclusive.

**Next Rnd – Beg V Neck Shaping**

With colours as for next rnd of chart, k4 steek sts; k1 edge st; ssk; keeping continuity of patt, work as set to the last 7 sts; k2 tog; k1 edge st; k4 steek sts.

Place a marker on each edge st to mark beg of V neck shaping.

Keeping continuity, patt the next rnd without shaping.

**Next Rnd – Beg Armhole Shaping**

With colours as for next rnd of chart, k4 steek sts and k1 edge st as set; keeping continuity, patt the next 40[42,44,46] sts (right front); place the next 11[13,15,17] sts on a holder; cast on 10 edge and steek sts (using alt colours for 8 centre steek sts); keeping continuity, patt the next 93[99,105,111] sts (back); place the next 11[13,15,17] sts on a holder; cast on 10 edge and steek sts as before; keeping continuity, patt the next 40[42,44,46] sts (left front); k1 edge st and k4 steek sts as set.

Working armhole steeks and edge sts as front, and keeping continuity of patt (make sure the elephants line up with those worked below throughout all shaping), shape V neck and armholes as follows—

Dec 1 st at chart patt side of front neck edge sts as set on next and every foll 3rd rnd. AT THE SAME TIME, dec 1 st at chart patt side of armhole edge sts on next 4 rnds, then on every foll alt rnd 5[5,6,6] times in all. 75[81,85,91] Chart patt sts rem on back. Then continue in patt without further shaping at armholes and continue to dec at front neck as set on every 3rd rnd until 17[18,19,20] chart patt sts rem on each front, thus working 100[112,120,133] patt rnds from above border and ending on rnd 16[28,8,21] inclusive. Keeping continuity, patt a further 1[2,7,7] rnds without shaping.

**Next Rnd – Beg Back Neck Shaping**

With colours as next rnd of chart, patt as set without shaping to the 75[81,85,91] chart patt sts of back; patt the first 19[20,21,22] sts; place the next 37[41,43,47] sts on a holder; cast on 10 steek and edge sts, using alt colours for 8 centre steek sts on two-colour rnds; keeping continuity, patt the last 19[20,21,22] sts of back, then patt as set to end of rnd.

Working back neck steek and edge sts as front and armholes, continue in patt as set, working the front neck without further shaping and dec 1 st at chart patt side of back neck edge sts on next and foll alt rnd. 17[18,19,20] Chart patt sts rem on each back shoulder. Patt 2 rnds without shaping and cast off all steek sts on the last rnd. 107[120.133,146] Patt rnds worked from above border, thus ending on rnd 23[8,21,6] inclusive.

With Cobalt [Ink, Ink, Ink] graft back and front shoulder sts together including edge sts.

**Front Band**

Cut open front and back neck steeks up centre, between 4th and 5th steek sts. With 3.25mm needles and Cobalt, beg at cast on edge of right front, and working into loop of edge st next to chart patt, knit up 57[65,72,81] sts evenly along right front to marker at beg of V neck; knit up 49[53,55,60] sts evenly along right side of neck to back neck holder; pick up and k the 37[41,43,47] sts from back neck holder; knit up 49[53,55,60] sts evenly along left side of neck to V neck marker; knit up 57[65,72,81] sts evenly to cast on edge. 249[277,297,329] sts. Joining in and breaking off colours as required, work back and forth in rows and patt as follows–

**Row 1 (WS):** With Cobalt knit.

**Rows 2 & 3:** * K1 Bronze, k3 Cobalt ; rep from * to the last st; k1 Bronze.

**Row 4 – Make 6[6,7,7] Buttonholes:** k1 Bronze, k3 Ink; * with colours and patt as set, cast off 2, patt 8[9,9,10]; rep from * 5[5,6,6] times in all; cast off 2; continue straight in patt to end of rnd.

**Row 5:** Work in patt and colours as set and cast on 2 sts over those cast off on the previous row.

**Rows 6 & 7:** With Burnt Umber knit.

**Rows 8 & 9:** * K1 Dark Green, k1 Burnt Umber; rep from * to the last st; k1 Dark Green.

**Row 10:** With Dark Green knit.
With Dark Green cast off knitwise.

**Armhole Bands**

Cut open armhole steeks up centre, between 4th and 5th steek sts.

With set of short double-pointed 3.25m needles and Cobalt, beg at centre of underarm holder and pick up the last 6[7,8,9] sts from holder; knit up 85[95,101,107] sts evenly around armhole, working into loop of edge st next to chart patt; pick up and k the rem 5[6,7,8] sts from holder. 96[108,116,124] Sts.

Place a marker at beg of rnd, and joining in and breaking off colours as required, work check patt as follows—

**Rnd 1:** * K1 Bronze; k3 Ink; rep from * to end of rnd.

**Rnd 2:** * P1 Bronze, p3 Ink; rep from * to end of rnd.

**Rnd 3 :** With Burnt Umber knit .

**Rnd 4:** With Burnt Umber purl.

**Rnds 5:** * K1 Dark Green, k1 Burnt Umber; rep from * to end of rnd.

**Rnd 6:** * P1 Dark Green, p1 Burnt Umber; rep from * to end of rnd.

**Rnd 7:** With Dark Green knit.
With Dark Green, cast off purlwise.

## FINISHING

Trim all steeks to a 2 stitch width and with Dark Green, cross stitch steeks in position. Darn in all loose ends. Using a warm iron and damp cloth, press garment very lightly on the WS, omitting border patt areas. Sew buttons to left front band.

## CHART

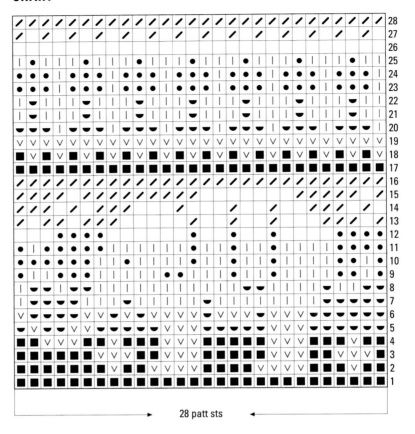

28 patt sts

## KEY

| | |
|---|---|
| ■ | DARK GREEN |
| V | BURNT UMBER |
| ➐ | INK |
| | | BRONZE |
| ● | COBALT |
| | GINGER |
| ╱ | VIOLET |

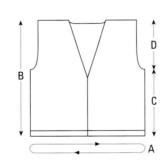

A = 68[73,78,82]cm

B = 33[37,41,45]cm

C = 19[21.5,24,27]cm

D = 14[15.5,17,18]cm

A phrase frequently used in our patterns is "keeping continuity of patt." It is important that through-out all shaping – such as neck and armholes – the pattern bands line up with those previously worked. Here it is plain to see that although the armhole involves holding and decreasing stitches, the elephants at each side of the armhole are still lined up directly with those below.

This photograph shows the grafted shoulder line, typical of our style of stranded colour knitting. The little borders clearly seen on armhole and neck are composed of a coloured Garter Stitch pattern.

# CLASSIC ARAN

'Twas brillig, and the slithy toves
Did gyre and gimble in the wabe:
All mimsy were the borogroves,
And the mome raths outgrabe.

'Beware the Jabberwock, my son!
The jaws that bite, the claws that catch!
Beware the Jubjub bird, and shun
The frumious Bandersnatch.'

He took his vorpal sword in hand:
Long time the manxome foe he sought —
So rested he by the Tumtum tree,
And stood awhile in thought.

And, as in uffish thought he stood,
The Jabberwock, with eyes of flame,
Came whiffling through the tulgey wood,
And burbled as it came!

One, two! One, two!
And through and through
The vorpal blade went snicker-snack!
He left it dead, and with its head
He went galumphing back.

'And hast thou slain the Jabberwock?
Come to my arms, my beamish boy!
O frabjous day! Callooh! Callay!'
He chortled in his joy.

'Twas brillig, and the slithy toves
Did gyre and gimble in the wabe:
All mimsy were the borogroves,
And the mome raths outgrabe.

JABBERWOCKY, from THROUGH THE
LOOKING GLASS by Lewis Carroll

As its title suggests, this is a timeless sweater based on the style of Aran garment that became commercially famous. Its appeal lies in its simplicity – both to knit and to wear. It is a comfortable, casual all-rounder. A honey-comb centre panel is bordered by plaited cables. The main pattern is worked in Seed Stitch, which gives the garment its crisp texture. A small variation is included – the lower border may be worked in Seed Stitch as shown here worn by Sam, or in a k1p1 rib as worn by Thomas on Page 78.

## SIZES

To fit approx age 2-3[4-5,6-7] years, or —
chest 54-56[58-61,63-66]cm 21-22[23-24,25-26]in.
Directions for larger sizes are given in square brackets.
Where there is only one set of figures, it applies to all
sizes.

## KNITTED MEASUREMENTS

Underarm 69[75,79]cm 27[29.5,31]in.
Length 29[33,37] cm. Sleeve Length 21[23,25]cm.

## MATERIALS

4[4,5] Skeins of **Alice Starmore Bainin** shown in Ruby
and Goldenrod.
1 pair each 4.5mm (US 7) and 5mm (US 8) needles.
1 Set of short double-pointed or circular 4.5mm (US 7)
needles. 1 Cable needle. 4 Stitch holders.

## STITCHES

**Seed Stitch:** Worked over an even number of sts as
follows—
**Row 1:** * K1, p1; rep from * to end of row. **Row 2:** * P1,
k1; rep from * to end of row. Rep rows 1-2. **Chart Patts:**
All odd numbered rows are RS and are read from right
to left. All even numbered rows are WS and are read
from left to right.

## TENSION

20 Sts and 32 rows to 10cm, measured over Seed Stitch
using 5mm needles. Measure the tension swatch
unblocked.

## FRONT

** With 4.5mm needles cast on 68[74,78] sts. Work
**either** Seed stitch patt **or** k1,p1 rib for 3[3.5,4]cm
ending with WS facing for next row.
**Next Row–Inc**
Patt 20[23,25]; (m1, patt 2) 3 times; m1 patt 3; (m1, patt
2) 5 times; m1, patt 3; (m1, patt 2) 3 times; m1, patt
20[23,25]. 82[88,92] Sts.
Change to 5mm needles and reading RS (odd numbered) rows from right to left, and WS (even numbered)
rows from left to right, beg at row 1 of charts, and set the
patt as follows—
**Row 1 (RS):** Work Seed Stitch over the first 20[23,25]
sts; work chart A over the next 13 sts; work chart B over
the next 16 sts; work chart C over the next 13 sts; work
Seed Stitch over the last 20[23,25] sts. ***
Continue as set and rep all rows of charts until front
measures 24[28,32]cm from cast on edge with RS facing
for next row. **Note:** All measurements of unblocked
pieces should be made along the center cabled pattern.
**Shape Front Neck**
Patt the first 31[33,34] sts as set; place the next

20[22,24] sts on a holder; leave the rem 31[33,34] sts on
a spare needle. Keeping continuity of patt, turn and
shape left side of neck as follows—
+ Cast off 3 sts at neck edge of next row. Dec 1 st at neck
edge of next 8 rows. 20[22,23] Sts rem. ++
Patt 2 rows without shaping. Cast off sts knitwise.
With RS facing, rejoin yarn to last 31[33,34] sts and
keeping continuity, patt 2 rows without shaping. Work as
left side from + to ++. Patt 1 row without shaping. Cast
off sts knitwise.

## BACK

Work as front from ** to ***. Continue as set until back
measures 27[31,35]cm from cast on edge with RS facing
for next row, measuring along centre cable patt. Cast off
the first 20[22,23] sts knitwise; k the next 42[44,46] sts
and place these sts on a holder; cast off the rem
20[22,24] sts knitwise.

## RIGHT SLEEVE

With 4.5mm needles cast on 30[34,38] sts. Work k1,p1
rib for 3[3.5,4]cm, ending with WS facing for next row.
**Next Row– Inc**
Rib 3[2,1]; * m1 rib 4[5,6]; rep from * to last 3[2,1] sts;
m1; rib 3[2,1]. 37[41,45] Sts.
Change to 5mm needles and beg at row 1 of chart, set
the patt as follows—
**Row 1 (RS):** Work Seed Stitch over the first 12[14,16]
sts; work chart A over the next 13 sts; work Seed Stitch
over the rem 12[14,16] sts.
Continue as set and inc 1 st at each side of 3rd and every
foll 3rd[4th,4th] row until there are 47[65,71] sts.
**First Size Only:** Continue to inc as set on every foll 4th
row until there are 61 sts.
**All Sizes:** Continue in patt as set without shaping until
sleeve measures 21[23,25]cm from cast on edge,
measuring along centre cable, with RS facing for next
row.
**Shape Saddle**
Cast off 24[26,29] sts at beg of next 2 rows. 13 Centre sts
rem. Continue in patt as set until saddle fits in length
along shoulder cast off edges. Place sts on a holder.

## LEFT SLEEVE

As right sleeve but work chart C over the 13 centre sts
instead of chart A.

## FINISHING

Rinse pieces in lukewarm water, then spin and block out
pieces RS up to measurements on schematic. **Note:**
Stretch the Seed stitch side areas on back, front and
sleeves, lengthwise to match the centre chart patts. Place
markers at each side of back and front 12[13,14.5]cm
down from shoulder cast off. Sew saddles along
shoulder cast off edges. Sew tops of sleeves to back and

### CHART A

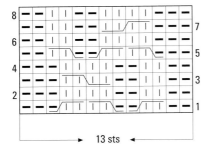

13 sts

### CHART B

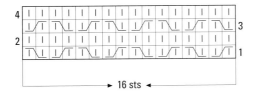

16 sts

### CHART C

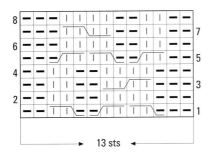

13 sts

### KEY

☐ p on RS rows; k on WS rows.

☐ k on RS rows; p on WS rows.

☐ sl first st to cn and hold at back; k2; p1 from cn.

☐ sl first 2 sts to cn and hold at front; p1; k2 from cn.

☐ sl first st to cn and hold at back; k1; k1 from cn.

☐ sl first st to cn and hold at front; k1; k1 from cn.

☐ sl first 2 sts to cn and hold at front; k2; k2 from cn.

☐ sl first 2 sts to cn and hold at back; k2; k2 from cn.

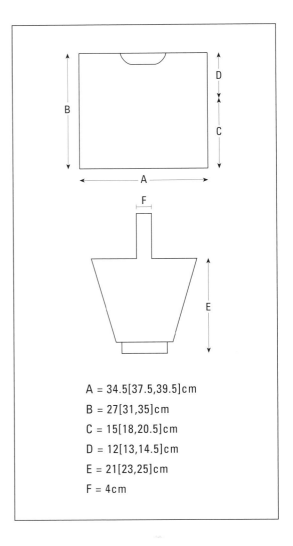

A = 34.5[37.5,39.5]cm

B = 27[31,35]cm

C = 15[18,20.5]cm

D = 12[13,14.5]cm

E = 21[23,25]cm

F = 4cm

front between markers. Press seams very lightly on the WS, using a warm iron and damp cloth. Use the edge of the iron to press the seams only, thus avoiding contact with the garment pieces. Sew up side and sleeve seams and press as before omitting ribs.

### Neckband

With double-pointed or circular 4.5mm needles pick up and k the 42[44,46] sts from back neck holder and dec 3 sts evenly over chart A & C cables and 4 sts evenly over chart B patt – 32[34,36] sts rem from holder; pick up and k the 13 sts from left saddle and dec 3 sts evenly over cable – 10 sts rem; knit up 10 sts evenly along left side of neck; pick up and k the 20[22,24] sts from front neck holder and dec 4 sts evenly over chart B patt – 16[18,20] sts rem; knit up 10 sts evenly along right side of neck; pick up and dec right saddle as left. 88[92,96] Sts. Place a marker at beg of rnd and K1, p1 rib for 6[7,8] rnds.

### Next Rnd – Dec

K 0[4,0]; * k2tog, k6; rep from * to end of rnd. 77[81,84] sts. K 4 rnds. Cast off sts knitwise. Darn in loose ends.

# CLASSIC ARAN

# SECRET GARDEN

MARY LENNOX had heard a great deal about Magic in her Ayah's stories, and she always said that what happened almost at that moment was Magic. One of the nice little gusts of wind rushed down the walk, and it was a stronger one than the rest. It was strong enough to wave the branches of the trees, and it was more than strong enough

to sway the trailing sprays of untrimmed ivy hanging from the wall. Mary had stepped close to the robin, and suddenly the gust of wind swung aside some loose ivy trails, and more suddenly still she jumped toward it and caught it in her hand. This she did because she had seen something under it – a round knob which had been covered by the leaves hanging over it. It was the knob of a door. She put her hands under the leaves and began to pull and push them aside. Thick as the ivy hung, it nearly all was a loose and swinging curtain, though some had crept over wood and iron. Mary's heart began to thump and her hands to shake a little in her delight and excitement. The robin kept singing and twittering away and tilting his head on one side, as if he were as excited as she was. What was under her hands which was square and made of iron and which her fingers found a hole in? It was the lock of the door which had been closed ten years and she put her hand in her pocket, drew out the key and found it fitted the keyhole. She put the key in and turned it. It took two hands to do it, but it did turn. And then she took a long breath and looked behind her up the long walk to see if anyone was coming. No-one was coming. No-one ever did come, it seemed, and she took another long breath, because she could not help it, and she held back the swinging curtain of ivy and pushed back the door which opened slowly – slowly. Then she slipped through it, and shut it behind her, and stood with her back against it, looking about her and breathing quite fast with excitement, and wonder, and delight. She was standing inside the secret garden.

From THE SECRET GARDEN by Frances Hodgson Burnett

SECRET GARDEN is a feminine, lightweight coat for girls. The body is worked in one piece to the armholes, and is subtly decreased to produce its A–Line shaping. Although not for an absolute beginner, this is a straight-forward design to knit. The pattern involves the use of the VERTICAL DOUBLE DECREASE (sl2tog knitwise – k1 – p2sso) which seems to confuse some knitters. There are two reasons for this confusion – both caused by misinterpreting the abbreviations. Firstly, 'sl2tog knitwise' means slip 2 stitches TOGETHER with the right needle in position AS IF TO KNIT. Secondly, 'p2sso' means PASS the 2 slipped stitches over, (not purl the two slipped stitches over, which is actually meaningless). If you have difficulty with this manoeuvre, please carefully study the drawings opposite.

This Lichen version worn by Amy evokes the Secret Garden of the famous story.

## SIZES

To fit age 2-3[4-5,6-7] years, or —
chest 54-56[58-61,63-66]cm 21-22[23-24,25-26]in. Directions for larger sizes are given in square brackets. Where there is only one set of figures, it applies to all sizes.

## KNITTED MEASUREMENTS

Underarm (buttoned) 66[72,76]cm 26[28,30]in. Length 42.5[48.5,57]cm. Sleeve seam 23[27,31]cm.

## MATERIALS

6[8,10] Skeins of **Alice Starmore Scottish Heather** shown in Lichen and Lacquer.
1 pair 4.5mm (US 7) needles. 2 Stitch holders. 1 Button.

## STITCHES

**Chart Patts:** All odd numbered rows are RS and are worked from right to left. All even numbered rows are WS and are worked from left to right. **Note 1:** Chart A shows RS rows only. On WS rows, k the sts worked in p on RS rows (as given in key) and p all other sts. **Note 2:** On charts B,C,D,E and F the patt worked over the centre 7 squares of each rep adds 2 sts per rep on row 2 from the 2 yarn overs worked on row 1, and 2 sts further per rep on row 4 from the 2 yarn overs worked on row 3. On rows 5 & 7, 2 sts per rep are decreased thus returning to the original stitch count. **Moss Stitch:** Worked on back and front yokes, sleeves and collar. Work over an odd number of sts as follows — **Rows 1 & 4:** * K1, p1; rep from * to last st; k1. **Row 2 & 3:** P1, k1; rep from * to the last st; p1.
Work over an even number of sts as follows — **Rows 1 & 2:** * K1, p1; rep from * to end of row. **Rows 3 & 4:** * P1, k1; rep from * to end of row.

## TENSION

22 Sts and 28 rows to 10cm, worked over Moss Stitch using 4.5mm needles.

## SKIRT

With 4.5mm needles, cast on 193[217,241] sts. K 2 rows. Set the patt as follows—
**Row 1 (RS):** Reading from right to left, beg at row 1 of chart A and rep the 24 patt sts 8[9,10] times; patt the last st as indicated.
**Row 2 & all WS rows:** K all sts worked in p on previous row and p all other sts – i.e. those sts worked in k on previous row, and also the dec sts, yo, and knot sts worked on previous row.
Continue as set and work through the 39 rows of chart A. Patt 1 more WS row as row 2. 78 Patt rows worked in total.

# THE VERTICAL DOUBLE DECREASE (SL2TOG KNITWISE – K1 – P2SSO)

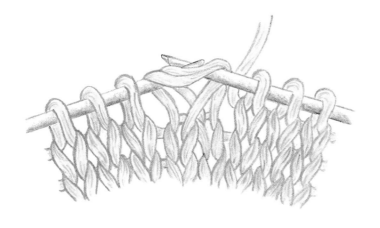

1   Insert the right needle through the next 2 stitches on the left needle, from front to back, and slip these stitches onto the right needle.

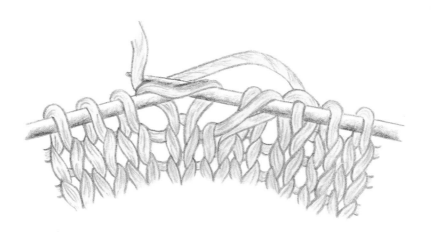

2   Knit the next stitch on the left needle.

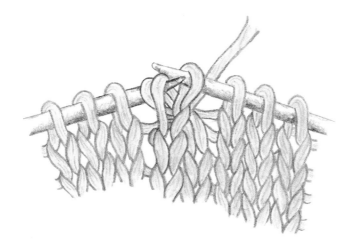

3   Pass the 2 slipped stitches over the knit stitch and drop them off the needle.

## Set Chart B Patt

**Row 1 (RS):** Reading from right to left, work the patt rep 8[9,10] times; patt the last st as indicated.

**Row 2 (WS):** Reading from left to right, patt the first st as indicated; work the patt rep 8[9,10] times. Continue as set and work through row 8.

**Second & Third Sizes Only:** Rep rows 1 through 8 of chart B once more.16 Rows of chart B worked in total.

## All Sizes – Set Chart C Patt

**+ Row 1 (RS):** Reading from right to left, work the patt rep 8[9,10] times, decreasing 2 sts on each rep as indicated; patt the last st as indicated.

**Row 2 (WS):** Reading from left to right, patt the first st as indicated; work the patt rep 8[9,10] times. ++ Continue as set and work through row 8 of chart. 177[199,221] Sts rem. Then work row 1 but **omit the decs** and k these sts instead. Continue as set and work through row 8.16 Rows of chart C worked in total .

## Set Chart D Patt

**Rows 1 & 2:** Work chart D, reading as chart C from + to ++. Continue as set and work through row 8 of chart D. 161[181,201] Sts rem.

## Second & Third Sizes Only

Work the 8 rows of chart D once more but **omit the decs** on row 1 and k these sts instead. 16 Rows of chart D worked in total.

## All Sizes – Set Chart E Patt

**Rows 1 & 2:** Work chart E, reading as chart C from + to ++. Continue as set and work through row 8 of chart E. 145[163,181] Sts rem.

**First Size Only:** K19; (k2tog, k19) 6 times. 139 Sts rem. K 1 row (WS).

**Second Size Only:** K14; (k2tog, k10) 11 times; k2tog; k15. 151 Sts rem. K 1 row (WS).

**Third Size Only:** Work the 8 rows of chart E once more but **omit the decs** on row 1 and k these sts instead. 16 Rows of chart E worked in total.

## Third Size Only – Set Chart F Patt

**Rows 1 & 2:** Work chart F, reading as chart C from + to ++. Continue as set and work through row 8 of chart F. 161 Sts rem. K 2 rows.

## All Sizes – Beg Armholes

With RS facing, work Moss Stitch over the first 30 [32,35] sts and place these sts on a holder (right front); cast off the next 8[10,10] sts knitwise (right underarm); work Moss stitch over the next 63[67,71] sts and place these sts on a holder (back); cast of the next 8[10,10] sts knitwise (left underarm); work Moss Stitch over the last 30[32,35] sts (left front).

## Left Front Yoke

Continue in Moss Stitch as set over the sts of left front and work the next WS row. Keeping continuity of Moss Stitch, shape armhole as follows—

* Cast off 2 sts at beg of next row. Dec 1 st at armhole edge of next row. Patt 1 row without shaping then dec 1 st at armhole edge of next and every foll alt row 3[4,5] times in all. 24[25,27] Sts rem. **

Continue straight in patt until yoke measures 4[5,6]cm from beg of Moss Stitch, with WS facing for next row.

## Shape Left Front Neck

**Next Row (WS):** Cast off 1 st; patt as set to end of row.

**Next Row (RS):** Patt as set to the last 2 sts; k2tog. Rep these last 2 rows 4 more times. 14[15,17] Sts rem. Patt 1 row without shaping, then dec 1 st at neck edge of next and every foll alt row 5[5,6] times in all. 9[10,11] Sts rem. Patt 3 rows without shaping, thus ending with RS facing for next row.

## Shape Shoulder

Cast off 4[5,5] sts at beg of next row. Patt 1 WS row, then cast off the rem 5[5,6] sts.

## Right Front Yoke

With WS facing, rejoin yarn to the 30[32,35] sts of right front and working in Moss Stitch as set, patt 2 rows. With WS facing, shape armhole as left front from * to **.

Continue straight in patt until yoke measures 4[5,6]cm from beg of Moss Stitch, with RS facing for next row.

## Shape Right Front Neck

**Next Row (RS):** Cast off 1 st; patt as set to end of row.

**Next Row (WS):** Patt as set to the last 2 sts; p2tog. Rep these last 2 rows 4 more times. 14[15,17] Sts rem. Patt 1 row without shaping then dec 1 st at neck edge of next and every foll alt row 5[5,6] times in all. 9[10,11] Sts rem. Patt 3 rows without shaping, thus ending with WS facing for next row.

## Shape Shoulder

Cast off 4[5,5] sts at beg of next row. Patt 1 RS row, then cast off the rem 5[5,6] sts.

## Back Yoke

With WS facing, rejoin yarn to the 63[67,71] sts of back and working in Moss Stitch as set, patt 1 WS row.

## Shape Armholes

Working in Moss Stitch throughout, cast off 2 sts at beg of next 2 rows. Dec 1 st at each end of next row. Patt 1 row without shaping, then dec 1 st at each end of next and every foll alt row 3[4,5] times in all. 51[53,55] Sts rem. Continue in Moss Stitch without shaping until back yoke measures 11[12,13.5] cm from beg of Moss Stitch (4 rows below left front yoke shoulder cast off), with RS facing for next row.

## Shape Back Neck/Shoulders

**Next Row:** Patt the first 12[13,14] sts; place the next 27 sts on a holder; leave the rem 12[13,14] sts on a spare needle. Turn and shape right side of neck and shoulder as follows—

+ Keeping continuity of patt, dec 1 st at neck edge of next 2 rows. Patt 1 row without shaping. ++

**Next Row (RS):** Cast off 4[5,5]; patt 4[4,5]; k2tog.

Patt 1 WS row. Cast off the rem 5[5,6] sts.

With RS facing, rejoin yarn to the 12[13,14] sts on spare needle and keeping continuity, patt to end of row. Turn and shape left side of neck as right from + to ++.

**Next Row (RS):** Ssk; patt to end of row.

**Next Row (WS):** Cast off 4[5,5], patt to end of row. Patt 1 row without shaping. Cast off the rem 5[5,6] sts.

## SLEEVES

With 4.5mm needles, cast on 37[39,43] sts. K 2 rows. Beg with a RS row and work in Moss Stitch, inc 1 st at each end of every 5th row, working all inc sts into Moss Stitch until there are 57[61,65] sts. Continue in patt without shaping until sleeve measures 23[27,31]cm from cast on edge, with RS facing for next row.

### Shape Cap

Keeping continuity of patt, cast off 4[5,5] sts at beg of next 2 rows. Cast off 2 sts at beg of next 2 rows. 45[47,51] Sts rem. Patt 1 row without shaping then dec 1 st at each end of next and every foll alt row 6[8,8] times in all. 33[31,35] Sts rem. Dec 1 st at each end of next 10[8,10] rows. 13[15,15] Sts rem. Cast off 3 sts at beg of next 2 rows. Cast off the rem 7[9,9] Sts.

## FINISHING

Block pieces, RS down, to measurements shown on schematic. Cover with damp towel and leave to dry. Sew shoulder and sleeve seams and press seams lightly on WS, using a warm iron and damp cloth. Place top of sleeve seam at centre underarm and centre top of sleeve cap at shoulder seam and sew sleeves into armholes. Press seams lightly on WS as before.

### Collar

With 4.5mm needles cast on 99[99,103] sts. K 2 rows. Shape ends as follows—

**Row 1 (RS):** Ssk; Moss Stitch to the last 2 sts; k2tog.

**Row 2 (WS):** P1; Moss Stitch to the last st; p1.

Rep these 2 rows two more times, working 6 rows of Moss stitch in total. 93[93,97] Sts rem. Break off yarn and leave sts on spare needle.

With RS of garment facing, beg at right side of front neck and with 4.5mm needle, knit up 27[27,29] sts evenly along right side of neck to shoulder seam; knit up 6 sts evenly from shoulder seam to back neck holder; pick up and k the 27 sts from holder; knit up 6 sts to left shoulder seam; knit up 27[27,29] sts evenly along left front neck. 93[93, 97] Sts. Turn and k 1 WS row.

### Join Collar to Neckline

With RS of both collar and garment facing, hold collar sts parallel and in front of neckline sts and with a third 4.5mm needle k the 93[93,97] sts of collar and neckline together. K 2 rows. With WS facing, cast off knitwise.

### Left Front Band

With 4.5mm needles and RS facing, beg at top of collar knit up 7 sts to cast on edge of collar, working through both collar and body edges; continue and knit up 64[78,94] sts along left front edge to hemline. 71[85,101] Sts. K 1 WS row. Beg with a RS row and work 5 rows of Moss Stitch. P 1 WS row. With RS facing, cast off purlwise.

### Right Front Band

As left, but knit up sts from hemline to top of collar and make a buttonhole on the third row of Moss Stitch (WS) as follows—

Moss Stitch 66[80,96]; cast off 2; keeping continuity, Moss Stitch 3.

On next row, cast on 2 sts over those cast off on previous row. Complete as left front band. Darn in loose ends. Sew button on to left front band.

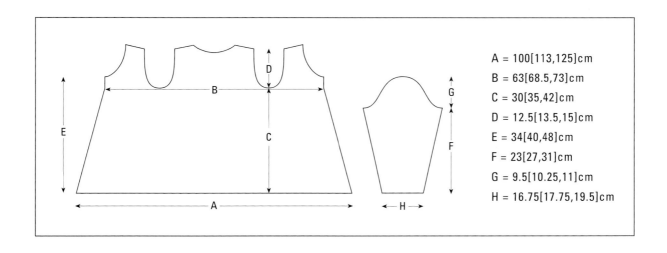

A = 100[113,125]cm
B = 63[68.5,73]cm
C = 30[35,42]cm
D = 12.5[13.5,15]cm
E = 34[40,48]cm
F = 23[27,31]cm
G = 9.5[10.25,11]cm
H = 16.75[17.75,19.5]cm

## CHART B

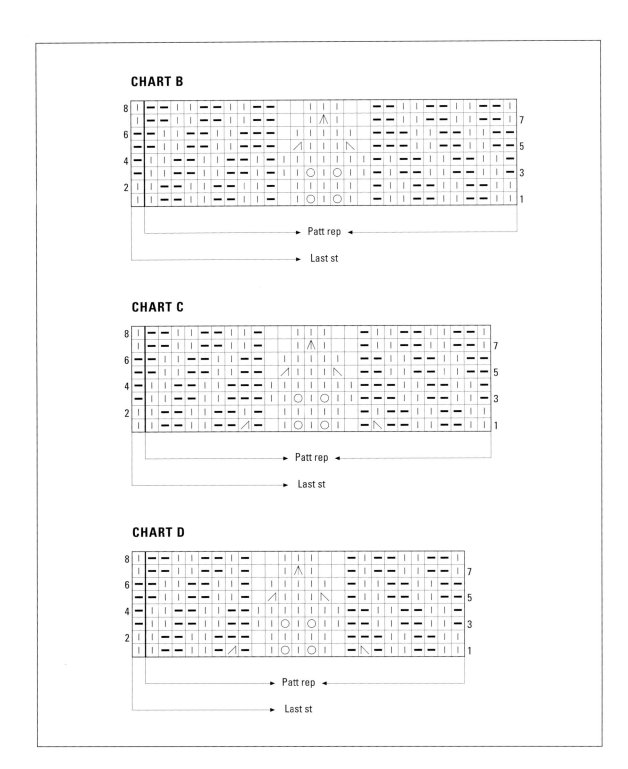

Patt rep

Last st

## CHART C

Patt rep

Last st

## CHART D

Patt rep

Last st

88

## CHART E

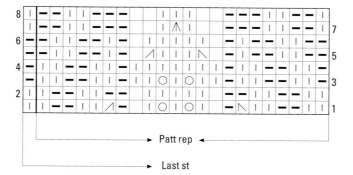

→ Patt rep ←

→ Last st

## CHART F

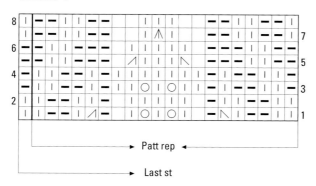

→ Patt rep ←

→ Last st

## CHART A

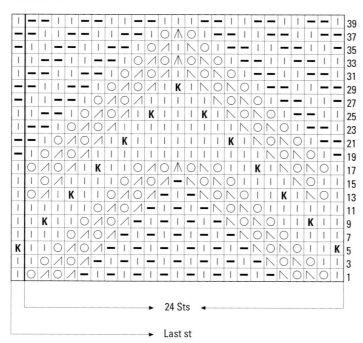

→ 24 Sts ←

→ Last st

**KEY**

⊟ p on RS rows; k on WS rows.

▯ k on RS rows; p on WS rows.

⊙ yo.

◩ ssk.

◪ k2tog.

▢ no stitch.

**K** make knot thus – (k1, p1) twice into same st, then sl the first 3 sts made over the last st made.

⋀ sl 2 sts tog knitwise; k1; pass the 2 slipped sts over the k st.

## SECRET GARDEN

assumes a more vibrant mood
when worked in Lacquer

# ABBREVIATIONS

| | |
|---|---|
| alt | alternate |
| approx | approximately |
| beg | beginning |
| cm | centimetre |
| cn | cable needle |
| dec | decrease |
| g | gram(s) |
| in | inch(es) |
| inc | increase |
| k | knit |
| k1b | knit into the back of the stitch |
| m | metre(s) |
| m1 | make one st by picking up the horizontal loop between sts and knitting into the back of it |
| mm | millimetre(s) |
| oz | ounce(s) |
| p | purl |
| p1b | purl into the back of the st |
| patt | pattern |
| psso | pass the slip stitch over |
| rem | remain(ing) |
| rep | repeat |
| rnd(s) | round(s) |
| RS | right side |
| sl | slip |
| ssk | slip, slip knit – slip the two sts separately knitwise, then insert the left-hand needle point through the fronts of the slipped stitches from the left, and knit them together from this position |
| st(s) | stitch(es) |
| st st | stocking stitch |
| tbl | through back loops |
| tog | together |
| WS | wrong side |
| yd(s) | yard(s) |
| yo | yarn over right needle from front to back, to make a new stitch |

# YARN
## INFORMATION

The yarns used in this book are available from the listed stores.

### ALICE STARMORE SCOTTISH CAMPION

2ply – 15 wraps per inch

28 gram (1 ounce) skeins

140 metres = 28 grams

500 metres = 100 grams

5000 metres = 1 kilogram

(150 yards = 1 ounce)

(2400 yards = 1 pound)

### ALICE STARMORE SCOTTISH HEATHER

2 ply – 10 wraps per inch

56 gram (2 ounce) skeins

110 metres = 56 grams

196.4 metres = 100 grams

1964 metres = 1 kilogram

(120 yards = 2 ounces)

(960 yards = 1 pound)

### ALICE STARMORE SCOTTISH FLEET

5 ply – 14 wraps per inch

100 gram (3.5 ounce) balls

225 metres = 100 grams

2250 metres = 1 kilogram

(245 yards = 3.5 ounces)

(1120 yards = 1 pound)

### ALICE STARMORE BAININ

3 ply – 10 wraps per inch

114 gram (4 ounce) skeins

156 metres = 114 grams

137 metres = 100 grams

1370 metres = 1 kilogram

(170 yards = 4 ounces)

(680 yards = 1 pound)

**ALABAMA**

**Yarn Expressions**
7914 South Memorial Parkway
Huntsville, AL 35802
800-283-8409
Website: www.yarnexpressions.com
E-mail: knit@yarnexpressions.com

**ALASKA**

**Inua Wool Shoppe**
202 Henderson Road
Fairbanks, AK 99709
907-479-5830
**Knitting Frenzy**
4240 Old Seward Highway #18
Anchorage, AK 99503
907-563-2717

**CALIFORNIA**

**Knitting Basket**
2054 Mountain Boulevard
Oakland, CA 94611
800-654-4887
510-339-6295
**Three Geese**
at Artisans' Co-op Gallery
17135 Bodega Highway
P. O. Box 362
Bodega, CA 94922
707-829-0931
707-876-9830
E-mail: Threegeese@aol.com
**Uncommon Threads**
293 State Street
Los Altos, CA 94022
650-941-1815
**The Village Spinning & Weaving Shop**
425 Alisal Road
Solvang, CA 93463
888-686-1192
805-686-1192
**Yarn Garden**
545 Sutter Street, Suite 202
San Francisco, CA 94102
415-956-8830
Fax: 415-956-8822
Website:
www.yarngarden.citysearch.com
E-mail: yarngarden@aol.com

**COLORADO**

**On The Fringe**
835 Main
Durango, CO 81301
800-547-7833
Website: www.onthefringe.com
E-mail: susan@onthefringe.com
**Shuttles, Spindles & Skeins**
633 South Broadway, Unit N
Boulder, CO 80303
800-283-4163
303-494-1071
**Strawberry Tree**
2200 South Monaco Parkway
Denver, CO 80222
303-759-4244
**Yarns +**
104 Orchard Avenue A-2
Grand Junction, CO 81501
970-245-2884

**CONNECTICUT**

**Finally Woolies**
78 North Moodus Road
Moodus, CT 06469
860-873-1111
**Hook 'n Needle**
1869 Post Road East
Westport, CT 06880
800-960-4404
203-259-5119
Fax: 203-254-7985
Website: www.hook-n-needle.com
E-mail: stuff@hook-n-needle.com
**The Yarn Barn**
24 Selden Street
Woodbridge, CT 06525
203-389-5117

**IDAHO**

**House of Needlecraft**
1314 North Fourth
Coeur d'Alene, ID 83814
888-775-5648
208-667-2822
Website: www.ewekknit.com
E-mail: ewekknit@televar.com

**ILLINOIS**

**The Keweenaw Shepherd**
202 East Westminster
Lake Forest, IL 60045
847-295-9524
**Mosaic Yarn Studio, Ltd.**
249 South River Road, Unit D
Des Plaines, IL 60016
847-390-1013
Website: www.mosaicyarnstudio.com
E-mail: mosaic@ameritech.net
**Weaving Workshop, Inc.**
2218 North Lincoln Avenue
Chicago, IL 60614
773-929-5776

**INDIANA**

**Cass Street Depot**
1004 Cass Street
Fort Wayne, IN 46808
888-420-2292
219-420-2277
**Heckaman's Quilts and Yarns**
63028 U.S. 31 South
South Bend, IN 46614
219-291-3918
**Mass. Ave. Knit Shop**
521 East North Street
Indianapolis, IN 46204
800-675-8565
317-638-1833
**Sheep's Clothing at Needle & Thread**
60 Jefferson
Valparaiso, IN 46383
219-462-4300

**KANSAS**

**Knit-Wit**
1815 South Ridgeview Road
Olathe, KS 66062
913-780-5648
**Yarn Barn**
930 Massachusetts
Lawrence, KS 66044
800-468-0035
Website: yarnbarn-ks.com
E-mail: yarnbarn@idir.net

**MAINE**

**Stitchery Square**
11 Elm Street
P. O. Box 773
Camden, ME 04843
207-236-9773
E-mail: stitchsq@mint.net
**Willow's End**
25 Townsend Avenue
Boothbay Harbor, ME 04538
800-242-YARN

**MASSACHUSETTS**

**Colorful Stitches**
48 Main Street
Lenox, MA 01240
800-413-6111
413-637-8206
Website: www.colorful-stitches.com
E-mail: mary@colorful-stitches.com
**Wild & Woolly Studio**
7A Meriam Street
Lexington, MA 02420
781-861-7717
E-mail: wwoolly@aol.com
**Woolcott & Co.**
61 J.F.K. Street
Cambridge, MA 02138
617-547-2837

**MICHIGAN**

**The Elegant Ewe**
400 First Street
Menominee, MI 49858
877-298-7618
E-mail: maa@cybrzn.com
**Knitting Room**
251 Merrill Street
Birmingham, MI 48009
248-540-3623
**Threadbender Yarn Shop**
2767 44th South West
Grand Rapids, MI 49509
616-531-6641
Website: www.threadbender.com
**The Wool & The Floss**
397 Fisher Road
Grosse Pointe, MI 48230
313-882-9110

## MINNESOTA

**A Sheepy Yarn Shoppe**
2185 Third Street
White Bear Lake, MN 55110
800-480-5462
651-426-5463
Fax: 651-426-5496

## MISSOURI

**Thread Peddler**
2012 South Stewart
Springfield, MO 65804
800-482-3584
417-886-5404
**Weaving Dept./Myers House**
180 West Dunn Road
Florissant, MO 63031
314-921-7800

## NEBRASKA

**Personal Threads Boutique**
8025 West Dodge Road
Omaha, NE 68114
800-306-7733
Website: www.personalthreads.com
E-mail: carolyn@personalthreads.com

## NEW HAMPSHIRE

**The Elegant Ewe**
71 South Main Street
Concord, NH 03301
603-226-0066
E-mail: elegantu@worldpath.net
**The Spinning Wheel**
2 Ridge Street
Ames Shop 'n Save Mall
Dover, NH 03820
603-749-4246
Website: www.nh.ultranet.com/~kurttoy/
E-mail: kurttoy@nh.ultranet.com
**The Yarn Express**
(Mail Order Only)
120 Moultonville Road
Center Ossipee, NH 03814
800-432-1886
Fax: 800-339-8509
**The Yarn Shop & Fibres**
549 Main Street
Laconia, NH 03246
800-375-1221  603-528-1221
Website: www.cyberportal.net/yarnshop
E-mail: yarnshop@cyberportal.net

## NEW JERSEY

**The Stitching Bee**
240A Main Street
Chatham, NJ 07928
973-635-6691
E-mail: stitchbee@aol.com
**Wandering's**
1944 Washington Valley Road
Martinsville, NJ 08836
800-456-KNIT

## NEW MEXICO

**Needle's Eye**
927 Paseo de Peralta
Santa Fe, NM 87501
800-883-0706
E-mail: needleseye@roadrunner.com
**Village Wools, Inc.**
3801 San Mateo North East
Albuquerque, NM 87110
800-766-4553
505-883-2919
Website: www.villagewools.com
E-mail: vwool@villagewools.com

## NEW YORK

**Amazing Threads**
2010 Ulster Avenue
Lake Katrine, NY 12449
888-SEW-KNIT
914-336-5322
Fax: 914-336-5361
Website: www.amazingthreads.com
**Elegant Needles**
5 Jordan Street
Skaneateles, NY 13152
800-275-9276
315-685-9276
E-mail: Eneedle@aol.com
**Garden City Stitches**
725 Franklin Avenue
Garden City, NY 11530
516-739-KNIT

## NEW YORK (continued)

**Heartmade**
(Mail Order Only)
877 East Tenth Street
Brooklyn, NY 11230
800-898-4290
Website: www.heartmade.com
E-mail: susan@heartmade.com
**Patternworks**
P. O. Box 1690
Poughkeepsie, NY 12601
800-438-5464
Website: www.patternworks.com
E-mail: knit@patternworks.com
**School Products Co., Inc.**
1201 Broadway
New York, NY 10001
212-736-3516
E-mail: berta@schoolproduct.com
**Spin A Yarn**
9 Mitchell Avenue
Binghamton, NY 13903
607-722-3318
E-mail: nrknits@aol.com
**The Village Yarn Shop**
200 Midtown Plaza
Rochester, NY 14604
716-454-6064

## NORTH CAROLINA

**Naked Sheep Yarn Shop**
120 West State Street
Black Mountain, NC 28711
888-250-3977  828-669-0600
Fax: 828-669-0675
E-mail: theyarnshop@mindspring.com
**The Yarn Studio**
901 South Kings Drive, #155
Charlotte, NC 28204
704-374-1377
Website: www.yarnstudio.com
E-mail: yarns@yarnstudio.com

## OHIO

**Wolfe Fiber Arts**
1188 West Fifth Avenue
Columbus, OH 43212
614-487-9980

## OKLAHOMA

**Mary Jane's Needlepoint & Knitting**
6413 Avondale Drive
Oklahoma City, OK 73116
405-848-0233

## OREGON

**Ann's Yarn Gallery**
11945 Southwest Pacific Highway
Tigard, OR 97223
503-684-4851
**Fiber Nooks & Crannys**
351 Northwest Jackson Avenue
Corvallis, OR 97330
541-754-8637
**Northwest Wools**
3524 Southwest Troy Street
Portland, OR 97219
503-244-5024
E-mail: nwwools@teleport.com
**Soft Horizons Fibre**
412 East 13th Avenue
Eugene, OR 97401
541-343-0651
**The Web-sters**
11 North Main Street
Ashland, OR 97520
800-482-9801  541-482-9801
Fax: 541-488-8318
E-mail: websters@mind.net
**The Wool Company**
990 Second Street Southeast
Bandon, OR 97411
541-347-3912

## PENNSYLVANIA

**Knitting Traditions**
611 Main Street
P. O. Box 421
Delta, PA 17314
717-456-7950  Fax: 717-456-5751
Website: http://members.aol.com/KnitTradit
E-mail: KnitTradit@aol.com
**Oh Susanna**
2204 Marietta Avenue
Lancaster, PA 17603
800-976-7282  717-393-5146
E-mail: ohsusannay@aol.com

## PENNSYLVANIA (continued)

**Wool Gathering**
131 East State Street
Kennett Square, PA 19348
610-444-8236  Fax: 610-444-8237
Website: www.woolgathering.com
E-mail: knit@woolgathering.com

## RHODE ISLAND

**A Stitch Above**
190 Wayland Avenue
Providence, RI 02906
800-949-KNIT  401-455-0269
Website: www.astitchaboveknitting.com
E-mail: NDarmohraj@aol.com

## TEXAS

**Yarn And Stitches, Inc.**
206 Spanish Village
Dallas, TX 75248
800-697-7567

## UTAH

**The Wooly West**
1417 South 1100 East
Salt Lake City, UT 84105
801-487-9378
E-mail: woolywest@sisna.com

## VERMONT

**Miller's**
106 Main Street
Montpelier, VT 05602
802-223-5281

## WASHINGTON

**Ana-Cross-Stitch**
713 Commercial Avenue
Anacortes, WA 98221
360-299-9010
E-mail: fishknit@halcyon.com
**Friend's Knitting**
17530 Island Highway Southwest
Vashon Island, WA 98070
206-463-4033
**Knot Just Yarn**
500 East Fairhaven Avenue
Burlington, WA 98233
360-755-7086
Website: www.knotjustyarn.com
E-mail: becky@knotjustyarn.com
**Spinner's Hearth**
7512 Lackey Road
Vaughn, WA 98394
253-884-1500
Website: www.onmy.com/spinnershearth
E-mail: spinners@narrows.com
**The Weaving Works**
4717 Brooklyn Avenue Northeast
Seattle, WA 98105
888-524-1221
206-524-1221
Website: www.weavingworks.com

## WISCONSIN

**The Knitting Tree**
2614 Monroe Street
Madison, WI 53711
608-238-0121
**Ruhama's Yarn and Needlepoint**
420 East Silver Spring Drive
Milwaukee, WI 53217
414-332-2660
E-mail: dawnann@gte.net
**The Yarn House**
940 North Elm Grove Drive
Elm Grove, WI 53122
414-786-5660
**Yarns By Design**
247 East Wisconsin Avenue
Neenah, WI 54956
888-559-2767
Website: www.yarnsbydesign.com
E-mail: yarns@juno.com

## WYOMING

**Threads 'n Tales**
215 South Third
Laramie, WY 82070
888-WYO-YARN
307-742-5282

## ALBERTA

**The Fiber Hut**
2614 - 4 Street Northwest
Calgary, AB T2M 3A1
800-816-7764/ 403-230-3822
Fax: 403-230-5699
E-mail: fiberhut@nucleus.com
**Wool Revival**
6513 112th Avenue
Edmonton, AB T5W 0P1
780-471-2749

## BRITISH COLUMBIA

**Craft Cottage**
7451 Elmbridge Way
Richmond, BC V6X 1B8
604-278-0313
**The Loom**
Box H, 4705 Trans Canada Highway
Duncan, BC V9L 6E1
250-746-5250
Fax: 250-746-5250
**Wool & Wicker**
120 – 12051 Second Avenue
Richmond, BC V7E 3L6
604-275-1239
E-mail: dianedebray@compuserve.com

## MANITOBA

**Ram Wools**
1266 Fife Street
Winnipeg, MB R2X 2N6
800-263-8002
204-942-2797
Website: www.gaspard.ca/ramwools.htm
E-mail: ram@gaspard.ca

## ONTARIO

**Four Seasons Knitting Products**
97 Southwood Drive
Toronto, ON M4E 2V1
888-388-6848  413-693-6848
Website: www.fourseasonsknitting.com
E-mail: jahunter@istar.ca
**The Hill Knittery**
10720 Yonge Street
Richmond Hill, ON L4C 3C9
800-551-564 / 905-770-4341
Fax: 905-770-8701
E-mail: dnimon@idirect.com
**The Needle Emporium**
420 Wilson Street East
Ancaster, ON L9G 2C3
800-667-9167
905-648-1994
Website: www.nas.net/~needemp/
E-mail: needemp@netaccess.on.ca
**Rena's Yarn**
18 Larraine Avenue
Dundas, ON L9H 6E7
905-628-4177
E-mail: mlduthie@hwcn.org
**Village Yarns**
4895 Dundas Street West
Toronto, ON M9A 1B2
416-232-2361
Website: www3.sympatico.ca/villageyarns
E-mail: villageyarns@sympatico.ca
**The Wool Room**
313 University Avenue
Kingston, ON K7L 3R3
800-449-5868
613-544-9544
E-mail: woolroom@aracnet.net
**Yarn Forward**
474 Hazeldean Road
Kanata, ON K2L 1V2
613-831-8027
Fax: 613-237-1585
Website: www.yarnforward.com
E-mail: comments@yarnfwd.com
**Yarn Forward & Sew-On**
581 Bank Street
Ottawa, ON K1S 3T4
613-237-8008
Fax: 613-237-1585
Website: www.yarnforward.com
E-mail: comments@yarnfwd.com

## QUEBEC

**Saute-Mouton**
20 Webster Street
St. Lambert, QC J4P 1W8
450-671-1155

# TO ANY READER

As from the house your mother sees you playing round the garden trees, so you may see, if you will look through the windows of this book, another child, far far away, and in another garden play. But do not think you can at all, by knocking on the window, call that child to hear you. He intent is all on his play-business bent. He does not hear; he will not look, nor yet be lured out of this book. For, long ago, the truth to say, he has grown up and gone away, and it is but a child of air that lingers in the garden there.

### R.L. STEVENSON